D1480838

Your Home Can Be Christian

Your Home Can Be Christian

DONALD MORE MAYNARD

Illustrated by JANET SMALLEY

A B I N G D O N   P R E S S
New York • *Nashville*

YOUR HOME CAN BE CHRISTIAN

Copyright MCMLII by Pierce and Smith

Library of Congress Catalog Card Number: 52-8841

G

SET UP, PRINTED, AND BOUND BY THE
PARTHENON PRESS, AT NASHVILLE,
TENNESSEE, UNITED STATES OF AMERICA

To My Parents
METTA MORE MAYNARD
ORVILLE KNOWLES MAYNARD

Foreword

$\mathcal{T}$HIS IS A BOOK FOR ALL WHO ARE CONCERNED ABOUT how to make their homes truly Christian. Newly married couples, parents, and even grandparents should find in it a clearer understanding of what is involved in making a home Christian. It faces frankly the problems of adjustment between husbands and wives. It deals as realistically as possible with the common, everyday problems parents face as they try to create within the family that atmosphere of love, understanding, and mutual respect which makes possible a Christian home. It seeks to help parents develop an understanding both of themselves and of their children, an understanding that carries with it insights that will make wise guidance of boys and girls possible.

Specific suggestions are given here for dealing with such everyday problems as eating, sleeping, getting along with other children, discipline, the fears of childhood, telling falsehoods, sex education, and the use of money. Special consideration is given to ways by which religion may be made meaningful to children, with suggestions about the prayer life of children, how to answer their questions about God, how to develop in them an appreciation of the church, and how to make family worship significant. Parents of adolescents will find throughout the book frequent references to the problems peculiar to that age, together with suggestions for dealing with them. Finally, since parents should take their responsibilities seriously, but must not

7

take them too seriously, suggestions are given for developing a wholesome attitude toward parenthood.

The building of a Christian home is a life-long task calling for patience, understanding, and religious convictions on the part of every member of the family. It is especially desirable, therefore, that fathers read this book, as fathers too are parents!

Grateful acknowledgment is made to the editors of the *Christian Home* magazine for permission to use certain materials of mine that first appeared within its pages.

DONALD M. MAYNARD

Contents

9

the home—securing obedience—methods of discipline

CHAPTER 1

But When Is a Home Christian?

THIS BUSINESS OF RAISING YOUNGSTERS IS MOST CERtainly a challenging one. There can be no question about that. There are plenty of joys and satisfactions connected with it too. If we are honest, however, we must also admit that the job brings with it many perplexities and heartaches.

We sometimes look back, almost with nostalgia, upon the time when we were free to come and go as we pleased; when the furnishings of the house stayed "put" after house cleaning; when we didn't spend hours over a hot stove cooking food that never seems to be adequate in amount. We can even remember when we were able to sleep late in the morning if we so chose, and in the evenings could run out to the neighborhood theater without bothering about finding a baby sitter, or, if our youngsters are old enough to go along, without making such a dent in the family bank account.

When such memories come back to us, they bring a sense of guilt. In our culture a person isn't quite decent if he doesn't rejoice in the opportunities and responsibilities that accompany family life. And so we go back to washing diapers or walking the floor at night with a youngster that has colic, and try to keep in mind how fortunate we are! We really feel that we are, too. If just those memories wouldn't be so persistent in coming back.

This sense of guilt is enhanced when we go to church and hear a rousing sermon on the importance of the Christian family, or when we attend the activities of Christian Family Week and discover that religious educators are tell-

11

ing us that the entire educational work of the church is largely dependent upon the home for its effectiveness. Of course we agree and we really hope that our own home is a Christian one. Deep down in our hearts, however, we are not so sure. In fact we are not certain just what it is that makes a home Christian anyway. We've heard a lot about the old-fashioned family altar, although we really haven't ever been in a home that had one. At any rate we don't have what we think is meant by one. So if a family altar is necessary in order to make a home Christian, we can't claim to have one.

Furthermore, if it is necessary for a home always to be

blessed by "sweetness and light" in order to be called Christian, our home doesn't qualify. Our youngsters tease and quarrel, even fight—not all the time, to be sure, but enough to make us feel sometimes that home is a bedlam. And although we don't like to admit it, sometimes we find ourselves irritated with our life partner. To be sure, most of the time things run smoothly, but even at best our home could never be characterized as one of perpetual sunshine.

And so again we find ourselves asking, "What is it that makes a home Christian?" We really want to know. We are tremendously eager that our children grow up to be Christian men and women, and we recognize that whether or not our desires are to be realized depends largely upon whether or not our homes are Christian now. But when is a home Christian? We welcome any insights that will help us answer this question.

When Religion Is Taken Seriously

Certain answers to this question are both obvious and exceedingly important. For example we can assume that in a Christian home the parents, at least, and the children, according to their abilities, will:

1. Believe in the God that Jesus revealed
2. Acknowledge Jesus as their Master and try to follow him
3. Engage in some form of prayer or family worship
4. Appreciate the Bible
5. Attend and participate in the activities of a church

It would be interesting if you would stop for a moment and recall your general impression as you read these five characteristics of a Christian home. As you read them, did you do so with considerable interest, or did you say to yourself, "Here's some old stuff," and find yourself rather irritated and bored? If the latter, it is not too surprising.

13

After all, these five are obvious, and the way in which they are expressed is trite. I am wondering, however, if you are bored because you are so adequately realizing them in your own home, or whether it is because you again are reminded that you are not doing so!

Whatever our feeling may be, let us not shrug off these characteristics with the comment of "old stuff." We need to realize with increasing conviction that we cannot expect our homes to be Christian if our belief in God is not such a vital factor in our lives that his will permeates everything that we try to do. If we are Christians in name only, so will our homes be Christian in name only.

It is right at this point that many of us need to pause and re-examine our own Christian faith. Many of us have grown up in Christian homes. We have attended church since our own childhood and have accepted, more or less without question, its doctrines. At the proper time we joined the church. During the days of our youth and young adulthood we found ourselves confronted with rather disturbing questions—questions such as, "Can we believe in a personal God in a scientific age?" "What does it mean to feel God's presence?" "What is the value of prayer, anyway?" and "Isn't the gospel of love impractical in today's world?" We may have received help in reaching satisfactory answers to some of these questions, but others we pushed aside with a wistful hope that perhaps sometime we would find an answer to them. In the meantime our religious life has become rather perfunctory. We "go through the motions"—perhaps have grace at the table, encourage our children to "say" their prayers, read the Bible spasmodically, and seldom refer to any aspect of our religious faith in connection with everyday experiences.

I realize the above description is not true for many of

you who are reading these words. Nevertheless I fear it is true of far more families, even church families, than we like to admit. However that may be, what I am trying to emphasize here is that if we expect our homes to be Christian our religion must really be meaningful to us. It must not be taken for granted in the home. It is not necessary, of course, that our conversation should be filled with pious platitudes nor that we necessarily should have the "old-fashioned family altar." But if our children *never* hear us mention God in connection with the happy or the distressing experiences we face, if they do not sense the fact that our faith in him gives us strength and patience and hope, it will not be surprising if they think of religion as primarily a "Sunday affair." If our own religion is "second-hand," the "thirdhand" religion our children are likely to get will probably be pretty skimpy and inadequate. An example of the importance of what I am trying to say is the testimony of an outstanding religious leader who said that the most significant religious experience of his childhood was accidentally seeing through the bedroom door his father kneeling in prayer. After that experience, when the father talked of the value of prayer, the boy knew that he was not uttering platitudes.

A Christian home, then, will be one in which parents do more than give lip service to Christ and his gospel. The particular way by which the family gives expression to its faith will depend, of course, upon the temperament and the past experiences of the parents. Let us not for one moment assume that the behavior patterns of Christian homes will be identical. They will not. Individual differences will be apparent. Let us not, therefore, feel either that we must duplicate in our own home the particular religious practices to be found in that of another, or assume that those families that do not follow our own pattern are less Christian than ours. It is not so much what pattern we follow, as whether or not we follow any pattern at all.

And now something else needs to be said. It is quite possible that some of you have been asking yourself if it is not possible for a home to possess the characteristics just mentioned without being truly Christian. Here is the family, for example, of a brilliant but stern Christian leader. The children in that home are reported not only to have no particular concern for religion but even to be hostile toward it. The father is known frequently to take his boy out into the woodshed and punish him so severely that his cries may be heard clearly by the neighbors. Granting that physical punishment may at times be justified and that parents cannot be held entirely responsible for the attitudes of their children, nevertheless there would seem to be a connection between this father's stern, unrelenting attitude toward his children and the fact that they have little respect for his religion. To be sure, they probably are compelled to participate in the family altar, to attend church and to "say" their prayers. It is clear, however, that this home does not reflect the fine spirit of understanding and comradeship that should be evident in a Christian home. By no stretch of the imagination can this home be called Christian, even though the five factors mentioned above may seem to be present.

When It Develops Self-Confidence and Trust in Others

What I am trying to say is this: If our homes are to be Christian, there must be something present other than specific beliefs or stereotyped religious practices. Important as they are, they are not enough. But what must be added?

Briefly, perhaps that additional something may be thought of as *that spirit of understanding and respect*

16

which seeks the finest possible development of each member of the family. In other words a Christian home is one in which each member is so surrounded by love and appreciation that he has a chance to become his best self.

This, in general, is the viewpoint expressed by George Stewart in his book *Can I Teach My Child Religion?* He maintained that every experience entering into the life of a child that enables him to develop confidence in himself and trust in others furnishes a foundation out of which that child can develop confidence in and love for God. It is especially important that we remember that the converse of this also is true. Every experience that builds into the life of a child a feeling of inferiority, insecurity, and hostility, or that causes him to distrust other people, makes it difficult for him to develop this love for and confidence in God.

Let no one think for a moment that what is being said here is a plea for spoiling our children or for making them self-centered and selfish. It is not that kind of self-confidence we are talking about. Nevertheless we need to remember the insight that students of human nature are increasingly giving to us, namely, that one who feels inferior and out-of-sorts with himself is basically incapable of giving love to others. It is difficult to have regard for others if one does not have regard for himself. And it is difficult to trust others if one has not had an experience with those who can be trusted.

It is not necessary, however, for us to take this viewpoint in its entirety in order to see its implications for this business of building a Christian home. We are reminded that it will be difficult for a child to believe that God does not have favorites if he lives in a home where his parents show favoritism to one of his brothers or sisters. It will be difficult, furthermore, for him to believe that God is just if he feels that his parents do not treat him justly. This is one reason why it is so important that parents discover wholesome ways of dealing with their children. When a child is punished hastily and unjustly by angry parents who have not taken the time to discover the reasons for his apparently undesirable behavior, he may find arising within himself feelings of hostility toward them and toward all that they stand for, including their religion. The less favored and lonely child, who somehow gets the idea that his parents care more for and are prouder of his more brilliant and attractive brothers and sisters, is likely to develop an attitude of bitterness toward life in general, an attitude that is not conducive to a growing appreciation of and love for God.

It is not necessary to multiply illustrations. What is important is that we realize that all the experiences of the family have great potential significance for the religious development of each member. This means that our task of guiding the religious development of our children is far more than that of talking to them about God and Jesus, reading Bible stories, or guiding them in a growing appreciation of prayer—important as each of these is. How much simpler it would be if we were teaching children religion only when we were talking about it! And how much easier it would be if all that was necessary to make a home Christian would be the practice of certain stereotyped religious practices!

When we discover that religious development is possible in all the experiences of life, how much bigger and more tremendous does our task become. Problems of eating, sleeping, discipline, emotional development, sex education, the handling of money, and the gradual cutting of apron strings—to mention a few—become more significant. To be sure, these are problems that are considered in any study of child development. Nevertheless we are going

18

to consider them in this book, always keeping in mind their religious significance. This is what will primarily differentiate this from other discussions on such subjects.

When Democracy Is Practiced

One final word. A Christian home will be run on democratic principles. There will be no one person to whom the other members of the family are subservient. Speaking crudely, there will be no "boss." Studies of happy families show that by far the greater number of happy homes are to be found when democracy, rather than autocracy, is the general pattern.

It should be remembered, however, that democracy does not mean the absence of authority. Neither does it mean that no direction will be given to growing life. Rather it means that authority will not be used for its own sake, but as a means whereby growing boys and girls may be helped to develop within themselves the inner disciplines so essential to personal happiness and to a well-ordered society. When decisions need to be made, the opinions of each member of the family will be considered. Children will be encouraged to make choices of their own. They will be given freedom and independence as they show themselves capable of using them wisely. The family council or something analogous to it will be used when family choices need to be made or family problems considered.

And so we see that the answer to our question, "When is a home Christian?" involves not merely the practices that we generally think of as religious but all the influences that affect the highest development of each member of the family. Recognizing this fact is a long step toward making our homes Christian, but we must see its implications in the specific situations of family life. We will consider some of the most important of these in the succeeding chapters.

19

CHAPTER 2

Christian Parents Adjust to Each Other

THE HAPPINESS OF THE HUSBAND AND THE WIFE IS THE most important single factor in determining whether or not a home is Christian. If they are not happy, it is inconceivable that in their home will be found the spirit and the atmosphere necessary for the fullest possible development of each member of the family.

Christian parents therefore learn how to adjust to each other. Although for some this adjustment may be easier than for others, even for the most favored it can scarcely be said to be easy. After all, when two young people marry, each brings to the marriage relationship habits, ideas, attitudes, prejudices, and ways of doing things that have their rootage in the past. Some of these have been discovered during courtship days; others will not be realized until the couple get into their own home. It is inevitable that differences of opinion will arise as the habits of one clash with the habits of the other. Adjustments will be necessary. And it should be remembered that they don't "just happen." They are made only as a couple sincerely love each other and are determined to make their marriage a success. Even then there will be many problems.

One of the first steps in the process of adjustment, therefore, is to realize that tensions are certain to arise and that a marriage is not going on the rocks because of an occasional quarrel. Let us not confuse an occasional quarrel, however, with the constant bickering and fighting that go on in so many homes. Rather, let it be remembered that it is important that a couple learn how to deal with tensions and problems in such a way that through them they will develop deeper understanding and appreciation of each other. Suggestions will be given later in the chapter as to some ways of dealing with tensions.

One of the disillusioning experiences of young couples during the early weeks or months of marriage is the discovery that there are periods, usually brief, during which one does not feel the romantic attraction toward one's partner that characterized courtship days. In fact there may be moments when one almost feels repelled by his partner. It is important, therefore, that both husband and wife realize that such a feeling of hostility is more or less to be expected and should be no cause for alarm. There is a sense in which we both love and hate the same person, and when the feeling just described occurs we are simply manifesting the reaction of normal individuals. To be sure, it probably would be unwise for us to greet our partner some morning with the comment, "This is the day I'm going to hate you!" Our partner might not understand! If we will not worry about the feeling and continue to behave outwardly as though we felt as usual, we may be sure that the feeling of hostility soon will be replaced by that of love and affection, which after all is our true and permanent feeling toward our beloved.

How many times during courtship days do couples assure themselves that their marriage is going to be different from all others. They are right, too. No two marriages are exactly alike. This means that so far as adjustment is concerned, factors that may be helpful to one couple may be of little value to another. For example, although in-laws in the home of newlyweds frequently are disturbing and tension-producing factors, in some cases they do more to preserve a marriage than to destroy it.

Emotional Maturity Is Important

Unique though each marriage is, there are certain prerequisites for successful adjustment that apply to all couples. First on the list, and in many respects the most important, is that of emotional maturity. Emotional maturity, of course, is a general term describing most of the desirable characteristics that one should have if he or she is to be considered an adult in every sense of the word. There are few who have achieved complete emotional maturity, but without having achieved it to some degree one is ill prepared to make adjustments to one's partner that make for compatibility and happiness.

One who is emotionally mature faces the problems of life honestly and courageously. A newly married couple may live in a dream world for a time after their marriage, but soon they must return to the real world in which they are faced with the problems of making a living, keeping house, finding new friends, and giving up some of the cherished habits of their more carefree days. They must each be willing to accept the responsibilities that go with marriage and the building of a home. In some cases this will mean living on a much smaller income than they had when single. In others it will mean leaving one's friends and locating in a new and strange community, with the accompanying homesickness and feeling of loneliness. In all instances it will necessitate an unselfish concern for the welfare of one's partner. During the days before marriage one may have been able to think primarily of his or her own desires and whims. Now there is always another to consider. One who is emotionally mature accepts with joy and appreciation the new life with its necessary restrictions.

If a marriage is to succeed, it is exceedingly important that both husband and wife shall have a sense of values that enables them to see events in their true perspective. There are going to be many small irritations, differences of opinion, and even embarrassing experiences that may assume far larger significance than they should if the partners do not possess this sense of perspective. Suppose your partner does squeeze out of shape the tube of toothpaste, whereas

you always have prided yourself on rolling it carefully from the bottom! Just how important is that? Burned biscuits may be embarrassing, but after all they are just burned biscuits and nothing more. Your partner may not accept your judgment as to the best route to take to reach a certain destination, but again, isn't it absurd to let the difference of opinion spoil an entire trip? A sense of humor and the ability to separate the significant from the trivial will do much either to avoid or to overcome many of the tensions that might arise otherwise.

Psychological Weaning

The importance of psychological weaning from one's parents cannot be overemphasized. When a young man and a young woman join their lives in holy matrimony, they pledge their all to each other, and from henceforth their primary concern is with each other rather than with the homes of their youth. One who is tied to his or her parents' apron strings is ill prepared for a happy married life. The

23

wife who runs home to mother whenever anything goes wrong, or who always contrasts her husband with her father—to the husband's detriment—and the husband who always has to get his mother's opinion before making a decision that affects his own home, are still children so far as their emotional development is concerned. Painful though it sometimes may be, couples must resolutely cut the apron strings that bind them to their parents. If it is necessary for a couple to live with one or other of the parents, it usually is far wiser for them to live with the parents of the wife than with those of the husband. In the latter situation not only are two women more or less in competition for one man, but the different methods of cooking and keeping house may prove an irritating factor to the women.

There are other evidences of emotional immaturity, all of which put a strain upon the relationships of husband and wife. Who is not acquainted with the wife who bursts into temper tantrums when something goes wrong and engages in "wooden swearing" (slamming the door); the husband who compensates for his feelings of inferiority by pouting and assuming a martyred air; the one who gets sick in order to get attention or to get out of doing disagreeable tasks; the one who is never satisfied with what she has, always looking with envy upon the homes of her friends? It is too much to expect that we shall completely avoid such evidences of childish behavior, but at least we can be aware of our childishness and constantly seek to develop that kind of maturity that results in self-control and inner disciplines.

This emphasis upon emotional maturity has been placed first in our consideration of the prerequisites for a successful marriage, as the emotionally mature are likely to meet the other requirements for successful adjustment.

Other Prerequisites for Successful Adjustment

1. *Genuine affection.* It is assumed that a couple will not get married unless they are genuinely in love with each other. Granting that the romantic thrills of courtship and honeymoon days must be superseded by the more durable, creative love that is necessary for the building of a home, it also is true that couples should do everything in their power to keep alive and vibrant their love and affection for each other. This will not be done by taking their love for granted. Studies of happy homes reveal that almost without exception the husband and the wife give expression frequently to their love for each other. They don't hesitate to tell their partner how much he or she means to them. They continue to give the compliments that meant so much during courtship days. They don't forget the good-by kiss. They delight in surprising their partners with thoughtful evidences of their love—such as flowers, candy, or an inexpensive gift. They remember anniversaries and make a gala day of them. They plan for "evenings out" together, even after children have come into the home. They avoid mannerisms or habits that they have discovered are irritating to their partner. In other words they make certain that the "romance" shall not be taken out of their marriage.

It is in this area of giving expression to love, however, that tensions sometimes arise. Here is a young bride brought up in a home in which, although the parents cared deeply for each other, overt manifestations of love were seldom given. Love was taken for granted. When she gets married, she finds that in her husband's home members of the family expressed affection freely, and he assumes that pattern will be followed in his home. She finds it difficult to be as expressive as he would like, due largely to her own home background. Unless this couple face frankly the fact that each will need to be sympathetic and understanding with the other and try to adjust in such a way as will be satisfactory to both, tensions are likely to develop. The husband will feel his wife does not care for him, and she in turn will feel that he is unreasonable in his expectations.

2. *Sexual adjustment*. Though sex is not the only factor in marriage, it is an exceedingly important one. A marriage based on sex attraction alone is not likely to endure, but a marriage in which there is not a mutually satisfying sex relationship is also faced with grave difficulties. If adjustments in this area are not satisfactory, adjustments in all other areas of married life are likely to be more difficult. Wholesome sex adjustment influences one's entire outlook upon life. Sometimes nervousness, a general feeling of irritability, despondency, and feelings of inferiority and sensitiveness may be the result of unsatisfactory sex experiences with one's partner. On the other hand these traits may be the cause of, rather than the result of, sexual incompatibility.

Couples entering marriage should realize that mutually satisfying sex relationships require skill on the part of both and in all probability will not be immediately realized. They will be patient with each other, therefore, and will not be discouraged if their first experiences are not all that they had anticipated. If, after a period of conscientious effort on their part, a mutually satisfying experience has not been achieved, they will consult with their physician or a marriage counselor in the effort to find out where the difficulty is. There are many excellent pamphlets and books that deal with the physical aspects of the marriage relationship. A few are listed in the Suggestions for Further Reading at the back of this book. It is helpful if a husband and wife will read these together. It always should be remembered, however, that the psychological and spiritual preparations for the marriage relationship are as important as the physical.

3. *Children.* Recent studies indicate that it is not so much the presence of children in the home that facilitates adjustment between husband and wife as it is the mutual desire for children. Couples who have unwanted children are likely to be unhappy and find adjustment difficult. The happiest homes, on the other hand, are those in which there are children whom the parents definitely planned for and rejoice in. Couples who discover that they are not going to have children of their own would do well to give serious consideration to the possibility of adopting a child.

Parents who have great love and affection for their children are drawn closer together by this common interest. Perhaps a word of warning is in order, however. Couples should not let their interest in the children take the place of their interest in each other. Sometimes this happens— perhaps more frequently with the mother than with the father. As the mother becomes engrossed in her responsibilities for the physical, mental, and spiritual growth of her child, she may tend to neglect her husband. No longer does she find time to give him the attention he craves. Or it may be that the husband's first concern when he gets home at night is the child rather than his wife. The child thus becomes a dividing rather than a unifying influence in the home.

Occasionally couples who are having difficulty in making the adjustments of married life are encouraged to have a child with the thought that the child will solve their problems for them. Although there may be cases where the advent of a child has brought maladjusted parents closer together, such an outcome is not at all certain; and if the maladjustment continues, three rather than two are involved. The risk would seem to be too great to make such advice desirable.

4. *Both similar and different interests*. It is exceedingly important that a couple should have many activities they enjoy engaging in together. Some of these interests will be centered in the home. Drive down the street of a modest residential section in almost any community, and you will find husbands and wives out in the yard mowing the lawn, putting out shrubbery, spading in the garden, painting the fence or the house. Were you able to get a good look at their faces, you would be impressed by the expression of content and satisfaction displayed there.

Interests and activities should not be confined to the home, however. Couples who never engage in community or church activities together, or never visit friends for an evening of recreation and fellowship, or never attend concerts or other cultural events, are likely to find that life becomes dull and boring.

Realizing the importance of having mutual interests, conscientious couples sometimes have a sense of guilt if they desire to participate in separate activities. Such a feeling is not merited. It is too much to expect that each partner shall not have some interests over which the other may not enthuse. In fact it is desirable that they should have differing interests, if they are not too many and do not interfere with the mutual interests they share. Because of them conversation will cover a wider range of topics and the contacts of the home with the community will be enlarged. A husband need not feel that he must like antiques, therefore, just because his wife collects them; a wife need not feel she must enjoy baseball games, especially doubleheaders, just because her husband finds joy in them!

5. *Skill in dealing with tensions*. Earlier in the chapter it was indicated that attention later would be given to ways

28

by which a couple may deal with tensions constructively. Each couple, of course, will discover how to do this in its own way. The following suggestions, however, may be of some value:

a) Try to avoid situations that you know are likely to create tensions. A couple soon find out those that are tension-producing, and by thoughtful care and determination can avoid many of them.

b) Be sensitive to the moods and feelings of your partner. When a partner is unusually fatigued, has had a difficult day with the children or at the office, or is troubled about business or personal problems, the other will make a special effort to be congenial, helpful, and understanding. By the same token, the one who tends to be sensitive and irritable sometimes can forestall difficulties by saying quite frankly, "Forgive me if I get upset a bit easily. Somehow I'm all on edge, and things bother me that ordinarily would not do so." Such a statement sometimes so clears the air that difficulties may be avoided.

c) When differences of opinion cannot be avoided and both feel deeply about them, frankly admit that you have a problem that must be faced. First of all, try to find out why each feels deeply about the situation. You will be amazed to find how frequently this sincere effort to understand the other's feeling creates an entirely different attitude on your part, and that which may have seemed so important no longer seems so. If it is discovered that one can yield more readily than the other, let that be done. Be certain, however, that over a period of time it is not always the same person who does the yielding. Be willing to compromise your differences whenever possible.

d) Try to keep a sense of perspective and a sense of humor. The two will do much to avoid and overcome conflicts.

e) Although it is important that differences and problems be brought out into the open, after you have discussed them and agreed upon a tentative solution do not bring them up again and again. Talk your problems through and then forget them. Don't make a debating society out of your home.

f) If you both find you are getting on each other's nerves, it may be that you are not having enough interests outside of the home. Perhaps you are not getting "baby sitters" as frequently as you should, so that you can get away together to visit friends, participate in church and community activities, or just go to the movies. Brief vacations apart are sometimes desirable.

g) Do not expect problems to be solved and tensions eliminated immediately. It will take time, so be patient.

h) Remember to take your problems to God in prayer. Ask for a spirit of love and understanding toward your partner. Pray for self-control and unselfishness and the ability to forgive and to forget. Christian couples cannot expect to avoid all tensions, but they should find in their religious faith that which will create in them the spirit and insights necessary to face them constructively.

i) If the tensions seem to be getting unbearable, counsel with a trusted advisor such as your pastor, your physician, or a professional marriage counselor.

6. *Religious convictions and affiliation.* From a purely theoretical standpoint it would be assumed that couples who are sincere Christians and are vitally interested in the church of their choice would be more likely to make the adjustments necessary for happiness in their homes than would those who make no pretense of being religious. It is very interesting, therefore, to find that studies of happy marriages tend to show the validity of the above conclusion. A study of over twenty thousand marriages, for ex-

ample, showed that marital failures were three times greater among those who had no religious affiliation than among those who were allied with a religious group. Other studies likewise show that regular church attendance is usually associated with happiness in marriage.

For the readers of this book it is not necessary to emphasize the importance of religion in building a happy home. It should be noted, however, that whenever possible, couples should go to the same church rather than the wife going to her church and the husband to his. Many couples report that a very happy compromise has been made by their joining a third church, that is, one to which neither belonged before their marriage. It should be recognized quite frankly that when a Protestant and a Catholic marry, the couple have a religious problem that is likey to be far more difficult to solve than that occurring when two Protestants marry. If religion has meant much to both of the partners, it will be difficult for one to change to the faith of the other. Nevertheless this is constantly being done, either the Protestant becoming a Catholic or the Catholic becoming a Protestant. If neither party is willing to join the church of the other, each of the partners will need to show tolerance and respect for the religion of the other, to have an understanding as to the religious upbringing of their children, and to seek for a sense of unity in their common belief in God, if happiness is to be attained and maintained.

CHAPTER 3

Understanding Why Children Act as They Do

$\mathcal{A}$s we turn now to our responsibility as parents, let us not forget the basic philosophy expressed in the first chapter, namely, that every experience entering into the life of a child that enables him to develop confidence in himself and trust in others furnishes a foundation out of which that child can develop confidence in and love for God. It is with this conviction that we approach the common, everyday problems that parents face as they guide their children.

For let there be no misunderstanding—most parents readily grant that they face problems in their role as parents. There are many times when they are puzzled by their children's behavior and wonder how they should deal with it. The following, for example, are but a few of the problems they list when given an opportunity to do so: temper tantrums, jealousy, selfishness, sensitiveness, lack of respect for elders, fears, disobedience, falsehoods, stealing, profanity, and difficult questions about sex or religion.

It is the assumption of this chapter, in fact of all the remaining chapters, that if parents are to deal wisely with their children, they need to have a growing understanding of the process of growth in general, and more specifically of the reasons for particular behavior situations. This is a big order, to be sure, and does not mean that one must be an expert in child psychology in order to be a good parent.

But neither is there any virtue in ignorance of child growth. There are insights that will prove to be helpful to those who think of themselves as average parents.

Parents will do well to keep in mind the following as they endeavor to fulfill their responsibility:

✓ 1. *They will not expect more of their children than they have a right to expect.* It is amazing how many parents expect of their children the self-discipline, unselfishness, and co-operation that characterize adults. It is important, therefore, that they shall come to an understanding of the normal behavior patterns at various age levels. As they do so, they will not be disturbed when their two-year-old manifests an attitude of negativism or when their five- or six-year-old shows his growing independence by being disagreeable and unco-operative. They will not be surprised when the three-year-old refuses to share his toys, or when adolescent boys and girls are moody, one day being despondent and the next exuberant with the joy of life. They will realize that these expressions of behavior are but the normal manifestations of the growth process.

✓ 2. *They will always take into account individual differences in children.* No two children are alike. Some learn quickly, others slowly; some are timid, others aggressive; some like to read, others are happy only in some more active occupation; some have inquiring minds, others seldom ask questions. This catalogue of differences could go on almost endlessly, as the parent of several children realizes. How frequently we marvel that two children in the same family can be so different in disposition and interests. But they are, and in guiding their development parents must take into account these differences. What is successful with one child is not necessarily so with another. Indeed, what works with one child now may not work with the same child a little later. A child does not stay the same. He is constantly growing and having new experiences. This simply means that nothing will take the place of "on the spot" intelligence as parents guide their children.

3. *Before dealing with specific behavior problems they will endeavor to discover the reasons for the behavior.* It should be remembered, furthermore, that these reasons are not always apparent, and that the attempt to deal with the overt behavior before understanding the reason for it frequently leads to unwise and sometimes unfair treatment. There are probably many parents, some of whom may be reading this, who recall having dealt hastily with a child whose behavior at the time seemed to merit discipline, only to discover later that had they known the reason for the behavior they would have dealt with the child quite differently. The following experience illustrates this point very clearly.

A father, coming home from work one evening, decided to take his brief case to the back bedroom and leave it there. As he crossed the living room, he glanced to his left and noticed his ten-year-old son sitting in the sun parlor working on a model airplane. He cheerfully called out to him, "How are you, Son?" Much to his consternation the boy replied, "Shut up, Daddy!" The father was tempted to rush into the sun parlor and deal in no gentle manner with his rude son, but decided to wait. As he walked down the hall to the bedroom, he felt hurt that his son should be so ungracious, and he also wondered just what he should do about it. His wife, having heard the conversation, said quietly to him, "Please do nothing until I have a chance to talk to you."

Later she told him what had happened that afternoon. A crowd of boys from the neighborhood had gathered on the vacant lot next door to play football. Some of the boys were older and much larger than the others. The older boys had been unmerciful in their criticisms of the younger boys, including their son. He, however, managed to control his temper, did not talk back, dug in a bit harder, tackled more viciously, and received innumerable physical bruises. During all this time, of course, he was feeling defeated, inferior, and was developing an attitude of hostility toward the others. Finally, without having given vent to his feelings, he excused himself from the group and went into the house where he could work on the model airplane, something he could do very well. All the time he was working on it, however, he was seething inside with the pent-up hostility of the afternoon. He was about ready to "pop." And just then "pop" walked in! When his father greeted him, the hostility of the afternoon had a chance to get expressed. The "Shut up, Daddy" was not directed primarily at the father; there was nothing personal about it. It was simply the expression of hostility that somehow had to get expressed.

Suppose the father had rushed in and punished the child without finding out the reason for the behavior. The youngster would have indeed felt that this is a pretty bad world. Not only was he unable to receive recognition and achievement on the playground among his peers, but also his dad did not understand him. What the boy needed was a father who would put his arms around him and say, "Son, I know it was pretty tough out there today, but I'm proud of the way in which you held your temper and stuck it out. Good for you. How about our going out and practicing with the football tonight so you will be able to do better next time?" What the boy didn't need was an angry father. At a later date the father might desire to help the boy see that even when he felt bad, he should not be rude to his parents. On the other hand, if this was an exceptional situation, it probably would be better to say nothing about it.

Basic Drives

As we attempt to understand the reasons for behavior, we must not forget that there are many factors responsible for it. The state or condition of the physical organism, the basic drives or urges, the past experience of the individual, the pressure of a particular environmental situation, and the goals or purposes one has set for himself are but a few of the reasons for behavior. Psychologists differ among themselves as to which of these reasons is the most important. Without our getting into this controversy let it be noted here that there are certain desires or urges that seem to have an influence upon behavior. Perhaps the most important are the following:

1. *The desire for a sense of physical well-being.* When one feels a physical need, he is restless until that need is met. If for some reason the satisfaction of the need is delayed, one's behavior is likely to reflect his sense of frustration. A tired child who wants rest will be irritable and cross if that rest is denied. It is the unusual child who will sit quietly throughout a church service or any other long service. His physical needs call for activity. As we shall note later, malnutrition or the improper functioning of the endocrine glands has a very definite effect upon the personality pattern of children.

2. *The desire for a sense of one's own worth and for the approval of others.* Two desires have been joined in this statement because the satisfaction of the first so frequently is dependent upon the satisfaction of the second. One of the deepest needs of mankind is to feel significant, to have a sense of one's own worth, and to have the approval of

one's fellows. The two- or three-year-old who turns somersaults in the middle of the floor when guests are present, the five- or six-year-old who brings you a drawing to admire, the ten-year-old who yells at you from his perch on the highest limb of a tree, the thirteen-year-old who

insists upon a permanent wave—all are but manifesting their desire for approval. All of us are seeking it, young and old alike, and if we do not secure it in the normal activities of life, we are likely to get it through phantasies and daydreams. Without a sense of our own worth and the approval of others we cannot gain that self-confidence which is so essential for wholesome personality.

3. *The desire for love and affection.* It is impossible to overemphasize the importance of providing our children with the assurance that we love and understand them. Sometimes we parents, especially fathers, become so busy with the activities of life that we take it for granted that our children know we love them. In one sense they do, but an occasional verbal assurance that is not gushy or sentimental is most reassuring. Without this assurance children may feel lonely, rejected, and become antisocial and resentful of all authority. Even the adolescent, with all his apparent indifference to his parents, desperately needs to

37

feel the security of their love. In happy homes members of the family express their affection for each other.

Although the needs just mentioned may be considered to be primary, there are other more or less secondary desires that influence the behavior of boys and girls. For example there is a great *desire for power,* as power usually gains one the approval of others, enables one to satisfy his physical needs, and brings with it a sense of one's own worth. Power may be achieved in various ways—through physical force, scholarly attainments, political office, or the respect of one's fellows. Neurotics frequently seek power over those they love through feigned illness. A boy implied he liked to play with guns because they gave him a sense of power.

The *desire for excitement* is a frequent factor in behavior. All of us are eager for experiences that break the monotony of life. If children cannot secure excitement legitimately, they are tempted to get it in undesirable ways. Thus not only harmless escapades but delinquent behavior may be the outcome of this desire. Which it will be depends largely upon the guidance the child receives.

The incessant questioning by children and their eagerness to get acquainted with their environment, especially the world of nature, root in a *desire to know.* Collecting not only adds to one's knowledge but brings approval, power, and in some cases excitement. Certainly to own or to possess something gives one a sense of power and satisfaction.

Reducing Tensions

In his various activities the child is seeking to satisfy these various desires. When something interferes with his plans, a state of tension is set up in his organism. He then tries various ways of overcoming the obstacles in his way.

If he is successful, the tension is reduced and successful adjustment supposedly has taken place. Conceivably, however, the method of tension reduction in one area may cause intensification of tension in another. For example, a child falls and hurts himself. He cries and runs to his mother for sympathy. This method seems to work in that it reduces the tension caused by the fall. Consequently the child builds up the habit of crying when hurt. As he grows older, he finds that his playmates laugh at him and call him "sissy" when he cries. This lack of approval in turn creates a new tension. The best adjustment is that which takes into consideration all one's basic needs, and the particular culture in which one finds himself. In the above case had the mother refused to encourage the child by withholding approval when the child cried, he would have tried other methods of adjustment and probably would have developed the habit of paying no attention to the inevitable falls and bruises that come during childhood. In so doing he would have developed one important quality of a desirable personality, that of facing bravely the hurts and difficulties of life.

Learning to Face Reality

In their effort to achieve a feeling of importance and to secure the approval of others, boys and girls sometimes refuse to admit personal limitations or failures. Perhaps the following illustration of this tendency may suggest to you an experience with your own children:

"Come now, this will have to stop," says a rather perturbed father as he pulls apart two angry boys who but a short time before had been happily wrestling with each other. "What's the trouble?" he asks. Scarcely does he get the words out of his mouth before both boys begin to speak at the same time.

"Jim pushed my face into the ground," says Jack angrily.

"I didn't do that until Jack kicked me," says Jim glaring across at Jack.

Patient questioning *may* secure from each boy the grudging admission that perhaps he had been a bit rougher than he should have been, but even then each is likely to insist that the other started the trouble. This is a perfectly normal reaction that some psychologists call *projection*, which simply means that one blames some situation or person for his own mistakes or failures. Most parents would be completely nonplused if a child should say, "I got into a fight and I started it."

This habit of projection, widespread though it is, means that those who engage in it are not facing reality. They are not coming to grips with their own limitations and needs, but are trying to maintain their sense of worth and status with others by blaming others for their own failures. Instances of projection are numerous and include such reactions as the blaming of the teacher for one's failure in a test, a blister on one's hand for striking out in a ball game, and other boys or girls for staying out late.

Rationalization

Projection is one form of what is called rationalization. Rationalization occurs when one attributes his behavior to reasons that both he and society consider to be good but which, although they may be partially responsible, are not the *real* reasons for the behavior. It has delightful possibilities in that by it one is able to convince himself that he ought to do what he wants to do, or that he ought not to do what he doesn't want to do. Boys and girls have realized these possibilities and take full advantage of them. One has only to listen to an adolescent's reasons for going to a show instead of staying home to study in order to see what a convenient mental device it is. It is interesting to note the self-righteous air of the daughter who after every meal must get right down to studying. Of course the fact that she despises to help with the dishes has nothing to do with her studious intent!

Rather frequently children, adolescents, and, yes, even parents become sick in order to get out of a disagreeable task. If boys and girls do not like their teacher at school, they may be sick early in the day and then miraculously get better by the middle of the morning. A child who apparently has unending energy for play suddenly becomes altogether too tired to mow the lawn. And what a boon a headache has been as a means of getting out of work!

The type of illness I have been describing presents a real problem to parents. For example, should a parent insist that a child whose illness he suspects is of this type go to school? If so, he may do the child an injustice as he really may be sick. A thermometer may help to determine this, of course. If the child is permitted to remain at home, he should be considered a sick child, kept quiet, perhaps put to bed, and probably given a restricted diet. If he really is sick, this procedure will be good for him; if his illness is an escape device, it may cure him. If, however, the child persists in having ailments for which there are no apparent physical reasons, his trouble may be due to serious personality problems such as fears, feelings of inferiority, or the inability to get along with one's fellows. The parent should discover what these are and help the child become emotionally adjusted to his present situation.

Phantasy and Daydreams

If the going gets too tough for a child, if he feels unable to compete with his fellows and consequently feels inferior, he is likely to run away from reality by engaging in daydreams. Through them he is able to realize his ambitions. If he is weak physically and in constant fear of being bullied by those of his own age, he may imagine himself to be a brave knight in armor, an outstanding football player, or a champion prize fighter. A girl who is plain and unattractive may picture herself as a beautiful movie actress. The chap who has difficulties in his studies sees himself as an outstanding scholar.

Daydreams are not always to be deplored. When they spur one on to greater achievements, they are desirable. It is when they are so satisfying in themselves that the child makes no effort to realize them in actuality that they are undesirable. Parents are wise who, when they note that their children are spending an unusual amount of time by themselves and are gradually decreasing the number of their social contacts, try to find out what they are running away from. The boy or girl who takes refuge in daydreams needs the help of understanding parents.

Compensations

Children, like adults, do not like to admit even to themselves that they have fears or feel inferior. In order to convince themselves and others that they are courageous and self-confident, they use various mental devices that are called *compensations*. For example, a child who is physically weak and who therefore cannot compete with success in games and physical activities with those of his own age may compensate for this fact by becoming a bully and teasing younger children. Or he may get satisfaction out of bragging about what he has done or can do, but which he never finds time actually to do. Sometimes such a child makes friends with one who is unusually strong and *identifies* himself in his imagination with this friend to such an extent that he feels strong too. Occasionally he minimizes his own weakness by ridiculing physical strength. One who has difficulty in his schoolwork is fond of asking, "Who wants to be a bookworm anyway?"

It is well for parents to be on the lookout for compensatory behavior in their children. A child who is overly aggressive, who always seeks to be the center of attention, and who expresses his convictions with great certainty may be trying to cover up a deep-seated feeling of inferiority. The child who is effusive in his manifestation of affection for one parent while treating the other parent with a certain casualness may be trying to compensate for a feeling of hostility toward the parent he clings to with such tenacity. The boy who brags about his physical courage and whose only interest seems to be in exciting adventure stories may be plagued by embarrassing fears. The stubborn child frequently uses stubbornness to get attention, assert his independence, and make himself feel important. The over-conscientious child and the one whom adults consider to be "perfect" may be using adult approval as a compensation for their inability to get along with those of their own age.

Compensations such as I have been describing are unwholesome because they are more or less unconscious and are the means by which one runs away from reality. Compensations which are deliberately and intelligently selected, on the other hand, may be the most wholesome way to adjust to many difficult situations. The boy who is physically weak, who frankly recognizes his limitations, and therefore seeks to develop skills in other areas—such as intellectual, musical, or social—acts wisely. The girl of plain countenance who admits she never can be beautiful compensates wholesomely when she seeks to develop an attractive personality and acquire the social skills and graces that will make her more popular than the "beauty" of the crowd.

What Parents Can Do

Let parents take seriously their task of helping boys and girls face reality. Let them realize that the ability to face life realistically is exceedingly important for mental and emotional health, efficiency and happiness, both now and later in life.

A child who is physically well, self-confident, able to get along well with his fellows, and free from abnormal fears will have little occasion to seek satisfaction by the various methods previously suggested. Consideration will be given, therefore, to these areas in later chapters. The best way to help boys and girls face reality is to make that reality so pleasant that they will not want to run away.

But let us also be realistic. Most children at some time or other get into some of the unfortunate habits I have been describing. When they do, what are parents to do? As children get older, we can help them see that they are running away from reality and why they are doing so. Insight into one's behavior is the first step toward the improvement of it. By sharing with our children our own sincere efforts to face life as it actually is, we may motivate them to do likewise. Through example and understanding we can help them develop "the courage of imperfection." We can suggest wholesome compensations for their limitations. We can give generous approval when they have the courage to face their problems and make sincere, intelligent efforts to solve them. When they fail to do so, instead of being scathingly critical we can assure them of our confidence in their ultimate ability to face rather than to run away from reality.

44

CHAPTER 4

Physical Health and Personality

*E*VERYTHING ELSE BEING EQUAL, THE CHILD WHO IS physically well is likely to be more mentally alert, emotionally stable, and spiritually sensitive than is an ill child. Mental retardation and emotional instability in children may be caused by diseased tonsils or adenoids, malnutrition, or defects in hearing or sight. In all homes, but especially in Christian homes, parents will be concerned about helping their children develop good physical habits.

Eating Habits

Most parents are properly concerned about the eating habits of their children, as they recognize the importance of right food for the building of a strong body. It should be realized that children from the more privileged homes may be suffering from malnutrition because their daily diet does not contain all the elements necessary for growth. Each day's diet, for example, should include the following:

1. *Tissue-building foods such as meat, eggs, milk, cheese, and fish.*

2. *Energy-giving foods such as sweets, butter, bread, cereals, and cream.*

3. *Foods that regulate the machinery of the body, such as vegetables, fruits, and whole grains.*

The primary problem of parents, however, is not so much what kind of food their children eat, as it is to get them to eat what they need, or rather, how to get them to eat what the parents think they need!

For example, here is a fond mother nibbling her own food and looking anxiously across the dinner table at her healthy ten-year-old son. "Now Jack," she says rather reprovingly, "you haven't touched that nice slice of bread I just buttered for you."

"But Mother," says Jack, "I just ate that big helping of potatoes you put on my plate, and now I'm full and can't eat the bread."

Mother, rather taken aback at the logic of her son's remarks, replies, "Well, at least you must eat your dish of peas and your salad. You know everyone should eat different colored foods each day." You see she has the rainbow idea of a diet! Furthermore, she has just attended a school on nutrition. But to continue with the story.

The father, having heard that it always is desirable for the mother and father to show agreement before a child, speaks up and says, "Yes, Son, do as your mother tells you." Jack rather grudgingly nibbles at his salad, takes one spoonful of peas, and soon asks to be excused from the table.

Don't be too surprised at the above illustration. I suspect something like this happens in many a home. It is comparatively easy, of course, to see what is right and what is wrong in the picture. The mother is perfectly correct in assuming that Jack should have a well-balanced diet. She likewise is correct in recognizing that it is not the quantity of the food but the quality and variety that give a balanced diet. And the rainbow idea isn't a bad one. She may or may not know that the personality as well as the physical welfare of the child is at stake. You can't build a wholesome personality on a faulty diet. Personality difficulties such as nervousness and bad temper frequently may be traced to malnutrition.

Here is a good example, however, of a situation in which a desirable motive is defeated by an undesirable method.

The mother, by buttering the bread, was encouraging in the boy an attitude of dependence upon her. Her anxiety that he should eat everything placed before him not only made her tense but made the others at the table ill at ease. Instead of the family meal being a happy occasion with every member of the family relaxed, it was an ordeal to get over. How much better it would have been had the mother placed good, wholesome, attractive food before the child and then stopped worrying about whether he ate it or not. If she sees to it that he doesn't eat too much between meals and is getting along well in his social relationships, she need not worry about how much he eats.

Parents forget that there are days, especially for pre-school children, when they need less food than they do at other times. Under such circumstances to compel them to eat more than they want may do more harm than good. Ruth Strang reminds us that forced feeding may cause digestive and nutritional disturbances and build up a sense of hostility between the parents and the children. She then adds, "Children who eat well are usually those who live in an atmosphere of affection and healthful routine and who have been introduced to new foods gradually and allowed to make their own choice, without coercion."

Granting that parents worry too much about the amount of food their children eat, it also is true that there are some very specific and helpful guideposts for them to follow as they try to get their children to eat. Some of these are as follows:

1. *Be certain they are ready to eat when they come to the table.* If they are tired or worried or have been eating indiscriminately between meals, they will not be hungry. This does not mean, however, that a light snack consisting of fruit and crackers is not desirable for children when they return from school.

2. *Serve meals on time.* Incidentally, many behavior problems arise when meals are not on time and children are "waiting around" for the meal.

3. *Expect your children to eat.* Some parents almost encourage their children to refuse to eat by saying, "Now I know you won't like this but it's good for you." Don't elaborate on the value of certain foods. No child wants to eat something just because it's good for him!

4. *Serve food attractively.* This means small portions, attractive colors, variety, and orderliness. Most children dislike messy plates on which different foods have run together. Small portions may lead to a request for a second helping and the sense of satisfaction that comes from the approval given to such a request.

5. *Have variety in the kind of food served and in the way of serving it.* Presumably one would tire of a juicy steak if served every day in the same way!

6. *Let the parents set a good example in their own eating habits, especially the father.*

7. *Let the table conversation be about pleasant matters.* The table is not a place for argument or the airing of family grievances.

8. *Don't nag, either by insisting that the children eat more than they want, or by continually criticizing their table manners.*

9. *Keep calm; be patient.* If the children discover that you are not going to worry about how much they eat, they are likely to eat more.

Fatigue Brings Trouble

Parents sometimes forget that personality problems are likely to have their origin in a state of fatigue. When a child is tired, he is likely to cry easily and to be irritable, non-co-operative, and stubborn. Every parent knows that quarrels between children are most likely to arise late in the afternoon when they are tired and hungry. For adolescents fatigue is a real problem. Because of their many school activities they are likely to neglect sleep. Because of their weariness they find it difficult to concentrate on their schoolwork, responsibilities in the home become a burden, emotional outbursts become frequent, and a feeling of inferiority develops.

It is impossible to state exactly the amount of sleep a child at a particular age should have, as children vary considerably in the amount of sleep they need. Ordinarily we assume that those six years of age and under need at least twelve hours of sleep a night; those from seven to thirteen, ten hours; and those in high school a minimum of nine hours. In many cases the adolescent, because of increasing growth and body changes, needs more sleep than eleven- or twelve-year-olds. The only way to find out how much sleep a child needs is to note if the symptoms of fatigue mentioned in the preceding paragraph are present.

Small children—that is, those six or seven years old and under—need a daily rest period, at which time they should be undressed and put to bed. If left to themselves, most children soon fall asleep. Parents should not be disturbed, however, if as children get older they rest rather than sleep during this period. If this is the case, let them have a toy to play with or some picture books. The period of quiet and relaxation is good for them, even if they don't sleep.

In helping our boys and girls develop good sleeping habits, let us keep in mind the following:

1. *The desirability of a regular time for the nap and for going to bed at night.* With small children no exceptions should be made. School children may be permitted to stay up a little later on week-end nights when they can sleep

later in the mornings. Do not yield to the teasing to stay up late on school nights.

2. *Children should be given a few minutes notice before bedtime so they may finish whatever they are doing.*

3. *Any excitement or hard mental and physical work just before bedtime makes it difficult to go to sleep.* Romping and exciting radio and television programs should be avoided; quiet games, family conversation, a story, or the reading of something that is not exciting should be encouraged.

4. *Children should go to bed feeling secure in the love*

and affection of their parents. Family difficulties should not be discussed just before bedtime, except when they can be considered without creating tensions. Avoid nagging.

5. *If children are hungry at bedtime, a light snack may help them go to sleep.* Avoid heavy foods.

6. *Never punish children by putting them to bed.*

7. *A comfortable bed that does not sag, proper ventilation, quietness, and darkness are essential for restful sleep.* Do not ask a child if he wants a dim light left on in the room. If he requests one, however, and can go to sleep easier with one on, there is no objection to his having it.

It should be remembered that worry and emotional excitement, as well as lack of sleep, produce fatigue. A child who is in bed the proper number of hours but who spends much of his waking time in attending exciting movies, listening to and seeing frightening radio and television programs, or reading unwholesome literature may be as constantly tired as the one who gets too few hours of sleep. For example, the following situations tend to overstimulate the three-year-old child:

1. *Being in crowds, especially crowds of adults.*

2. *Too many trips or excursions.* Museums, unusually large zoos, circuses, and carnivals are likely to be confusing to a three-year-old, and thus overstimulating.

3. *Movies, practically all of them.* Even cartoons can be too exciting.

4. *Fairy stories that include accounts of cruel men and women.* On the other hand children of this age delight in personalized animal stories.

5. *Exciting radio and television programs.*

6. *Toys that are too difficult for them, such as those that require the exercise of the small rather than the large muscles.* Mechanical toys that require winding and that get broken easily are undesirable for children of this age.

7. *Teasing by adults.*

8. *Quarreling parents.* If a three-year-old senses that his parents are angry with each other, his sense of security is lessened, and he is likely to become fearful and irritable.

9. *Hearing about serious illness or death.* A three-year-old can develop fears of sickness and death even though their meaning may not be too clear to him.

Let us remember, therefore, that if we permit our children to stay tired most of the time, we may assuredly expect to have difficulty with them. Furthermore we should remember that they will be developing unwholesome patterns of behavior that will be difficult to overcome.

The Endocrine Glands

Much is being written about the influence of endocrine glands upon personality and behavior. Although we must not be misled by the enthusiastic claims of those who insist that personality traits are *entirely* the result of glandular functioning, neither should we minimize the part these glands do play in behavior. If a child is unusually active or nervous or irritable, a basal metabolism test may reveal that his thyroid gland is secreting excessive amounts of its hormone into the blood stream. On the other hand, if he is sluggish, lacks a normal interest in what goes on about him, and is generally lacking in physical energy, it may be that not enough thyroxin is getting into the blood stream. If the child's sex development is not normal, glandular disturbances may be responsible for the condition. An unusual amount of fat, especially in boys, may be due to a pituitary disorder. When this is the cause, the boy is likely to be weak physically and to be considered a "sissy" by his comrades. This in turn gives him a feeling of insecurity.

Whereas glandular disorders are not the only cause of personality disorders, they may be *a* cause. A wise parent therefore will have his child given a basal metabolism test if his personality problems are unusual.

Physical Handicaps

Physical handicaps are likely to affect a child's personality. Nearsighted children who find it difficult to compete with others on the playground may develop feelings of inferiority which in turn may lead to timidity and quarrelsomeness. Children who are deaf are likely to be inattentive, to have difficulty in pronouncing common words, to make mistakes in carrying out instructions, and thus appear to be dull. It is no wonder, therefore, that their faces bear a wearied expression before the day is over, and that they are more poorly adjusted emotionally than those whose hearing is normal.

Crippled children are unusually handicapped in their struggle to achieve a wholesome personality. Adults unthinkingly express pity for them, protect and coddle them until they find it easy to assume that the world owes them ease and comfort. A crippled young man told his college instructor that the most significant moment of his childhood occurred when one of his teachers asked him to mail a letter. Other boys in the room remonstrated, offering to run the errand for him. The teacher refused their offers, saying he—the crippled boy—could mail it as well as they could. If we would keep handicapped children from becoming self-centered, demanding, and unhappy, we will avoid expressing pity for them and will treat them as nearly as possible as if they were normal.

Here is a wise mother seeking suggestions as to how she may in the years ahead make life easier for her eighteen-month-old daughter who was born with a red birthmark covering her right hand and arm. Already, when they take her out, other children are asking, "What's that?" or,

"What makes her hand so red?" This mother should realize that probably the most important factor in the situation is her own attitude and that of other members of the family. If she and they can accept the birthmark without bitterness or embarrassment, if it is not thought of as something of which to be ashamed, it is quite likely that their attitudes will become the attitude of the daughter. Her first task, then, is with herself—to accept the birthmark as unfortunate, yes, but not as something that in any sense need ruin one's life.

Having accepted the situation herself, she will be in a better position to help the daughter face it as she gets older and notices the birthmark. When the daughter gets to the place where she notices the mark and the stares or comments of others, the mother may want to talk with her quite frankly and unemotionally about it. She should be given the medical explanation of the mark, even though she may not fully understand it. If children ask her about it, she may even get to the place where she can refer to the redness as being caused by a concentration of red blood cells! Certainly there should be no reason for being ashamed or embarrassed because of it.

Nevertheless it is inevitable that there will be times when the daughter will be a bit irked and embarrassed because of the attention the arm receives. She may be tempted to engage in self-pity and even to feel rather hostile toward the world in general. When these occasions occur, the mother should be understanding and patient, letting her know that she realizes that sometimes it is pretty "tough to take" but that she has confidence in her ability to "take it."

Many a parent in his attempt to bring physical health to a sick child makes of him an emotional cripple. He lets him have his own way, gets him anything he wants, makes but few demands upon him, with the result that the child becomes self-centered, irresponsible, and thoroughly spoiled. Such a child may become the kind of adult who gets sick whenever he faces a difficult task, when he can't have his own way, or when he feels he isn't getting the attention he deserves.

Stature Makes a Difference

There is some evidence that physical stature has an influence upon personality. Smallness in stature, especially in men, is likely to produce a feeling of inferiority. In order to overcome this feeling the short person often becomes aggressive and active in his social relationships. On the other hand, one who is tall and of fine physique is likely to command attention and respect. Consequently his self-confidence is of the quiet, impressive sort rather than of the aggressive, vocal type. Occasionally, however, one who is unusually tall feels conspicuous and, disliking attention, becomes timid and shy. Unusual height is a special problem for girls. The mother of an unusually tall high-school girl tells of the unwillingness of the girl to go to social affairs where all the boys were so much shorter than she. The mother's laughing remark that she thought she would have a party for her daughter and invite only tall boys had some merit. Adults should remember, too, that adolescent boys and girls do not like to be reminded of their size, or of how much they have grown.

CHAPTER 5

Helping Children Develop Self-Confidence

IT IS ALMOST IMPOSSIBLE TO EXAGGERATE THE IMPORtance of helping boys and girls achieve emotional stability. Their own personal happiness and that of their friends and loved ones, their chance in later life for a happy home of their own, for vocational success, and for a worth-while and honored place in the life of the community, depend largely upon the extent to which they develop emotional poise and self-control and upon whether they have self-confidence, an appreciation of and ability to work with others, and a faith in God.

Although in this chapter we are going to give special consideration to ways of helping children develop self-confidence, it should be remembered that in a very real sense the suggestions in the other chapters are pertinent for this development. An example is the discussion of the contribution of physical health to the building of a wholesome personality. Later considerations of helping children learn how to get along with others, of wholesome sex education, and of growing spiritual insights will be dealing with important factors in the building of self-confidence, also.

Let us approach this problem of self-confidence by referring to the rather impatient remark of a nine-year-old boy to the suggestion of his father that he make a special effort to be friendly to a new boy in his class. "But Dad, he's such a sissy; he won't play any rough games, and yet picks on you when he thinks he can get away with it."

Overprotection

This was the situation. The new boy, not strong physically, was met by his mother each morning at the recess period, and they went walking together while the other boys played on the playground. A devoted mother! Perhaps, but also an exceedingly foolish one. In protecting her son from possible physical mishaps on the playground she was laying the foundation for emotional maladjustments that would interfere with the development of a wholesome personality. Of course the boy lost confidence in himself. In his attempt to cover up his feeling of inferiority and to get attention he would pick on the other boys. They soon discovered that if they in turn bothered him, they were rebuked by the teacher. Their dislike for the boy, therefore, was quite understandable.

The primary purpose of this illustration is to stress the fact that parents who are concerned that their children develop self-confidence should guard against overprotection. This overprotection may express itself in various ways. It may cause a parent to keep the child from any situation that in any way involves physical danger. Consequently he may be deprived of some of the most satisfying experiences of childhood. There are certain risks in most games such as football, basketball, or baseball. The climbing of trees, one of the most joyous experiences of childhood, always includes the possibility of a disastrous fall. The trip of exploration to the big creek or the woods may end in a sprained ankle or a snake bite. Even an apparently harmless trip on a bicycle may lead to a serious accident. If we forbid these normal activities, the child becomes hesitant and fearful, his companions think him to be queer, and we have a real behavior problem on our hands.

What we are now emphasizing is overprotection, not *protection*. A mother asks if it is wise to have a fence around the yard to keep her three-year-old child from wandering out into a rather heavily traveled highway that passes her house. Most certainly it is. It is our responsibility to protect our children from situations that obviously are too dangerous. At the same time let us constantly guard against overprotection.

Encourage Independence

Overprotection may take the form of the parent's making most of the decisions for a child and protecting him from the consequences of those that he does make. If we would have our boys and girls become self-confident, we must begin early to create in them a feeling of independence. We should encourage them to make their own decisions and, except in cases where the results would be exceedingly disastrous, let them face and experience the results. Children who are taken into the family council, who have a part in determining family plans and procedure, who have an allowance they can spend as they desire, and who have learned to make up their minds and abide by the consequences of their decisions are securing the finest kind of foundation for a wholesome, self-confident attitude toward life.

Don't Expect Too Much

Parents' expectations may either help or hinder the development of self-confidence. When parents have confidence in the moral integrity of their children and show it by trusting them, they help their children feel a sense of their own worth. It was in rueful tones that an adolescent boy said, "My aunt always expected the worst of me so I tried not to disappoint her."

Furthermore, when parents show their confidence in a child by assuming that he has done his best, whether it be in the schoolroom or in any other situation in life, they spur him on to greater achievements. They do not hold out impossible goals for him to reach. They are not disappointed if he doesn't achieve what some other member of the family has achieved. They evaluate him in the light of his own abilities.

On the other hand, when parents' expectations are too high, the child is made to feel so acutely their desire for his success in the schoolroom, on the athletic field, or in social life that he becomes tense and nervous. The strain of reaching beyond his capacity will be harmful. If he fails, and one is certain to fail occasionally, he has a sense of guilt and loses confidence in his own ability. He is disturbed, furthermore, by the feeling of resentment toward his parents that is developing. It is the thoughtless parent who, when his child goes to school, says, "Now, I expect nothing but A's on your report card," or, "When I was in school, I was a 'shark' in arithmetic. Don't you spoil the family record." It is a sick and lonely boy who feels his father's disappointment in him because he didn't make the athletic team. It is a tortured spirit who hears her mother say, "Why can't you be popular like other girls?"

Many a young man has been sentenced to a lifelong feeling of inferiority and dissatisfaction because he has permitted his parents to force him into a vocation that holds little interest for him and for which he has no special aptitude. A tragic example of this was the young man of slow mentality who struggled through college in an effort to become a lawyer, whereas his real interest was in the hotel business. His family, he said, insisted that he go into a profession, as that was in accord with the family tradition. Fathers who are wise will help their children select intelligently their vocation but will guard against forcing them into any particular one.

Avoid Comparisons

Parents should have emblazoned upon their consciousness and conscience these words, *avoid comparisons!* Nothing quite takes the zest out of life so quickly, or destroys initiative so completely, as to be compared adversely with another. The favored child is likely to become smug and complacent, whereas the less favored one tends to become discouraged and morose. The second child in a family is especially likely to develop a feeling of inferiority. As he plays in the sand, works with modeling clay, draws, or engages in athletic activities, he finds himself at a disadvantage. His older brother or sister can do so much better than he. Unless he is encouraged and given approval for his work, and helped to see that he must not compare his work with that of an older child, he is likely to become discouraged and to lose confidence in himself. It was a good omen when a six-year-old brought to his father a drawing and said, "Daddy, don't you think this is pretty good for a six-year-old?"

A rather plain, unattractive, and timid college student sought counsel as to how she might develop ease in social gatherings. During high-school days, it seems, her younger, more attractive sister was very popular and had many dates. She, on the other hand, seldom had a date, and students more or less ignored her. Instead of seeking ways by which they might help her make a place for herself in the school, her parents chided and scolded her for not getting out and being popular "like your sister." Their lack of understanding left her hurt, bewildered, and feeling very insecure. "If Mother and Dad don't understand how hard it is to compete with Mary, what's the use?" was the agonizing cry of this very lonely girl. She became increasingly timid and fearful in social groups. The parents had done a thorough job in ruining her self-confidence.

Strive as we may to avoid comparisons, it is inevitable that in a family where there are several children, situations will arise in which the differences in the children are apparent, even though no particular attention may be called to them. Boys and girls are not blind. They sense the fact that one may be more mentally alert and another more personally attractive. Fortunately, however, every child has certain elements of strength that the others do not have. Let us recognize these and build up in the thinking of the family group the realization that not all are alike, but that each one has abilities and talents that will enable him to make life successful and worth while.

For example, our children bring report cards home. One has all A's, the other all B's, and the third all C's. How are we going to handle the situation so the third child doesn't develop a feeling of inferiority and also a feeling of hostility toward those who received A's and B's? If each grade represents the best efforts of the child, we will of course give equal approval to all. In addition, however, it will be necessary to remind the third child from time to time that he equals or excels his brothers and sisters in other areas—possibly athletic or musical skills. The basic principle to keep in mind is that all comparisons should be with one's past accomplishments rather than with other persons.

Here is a four-year-old girl whose hair is quite straight, whereas her two-year-old sister's hair is blond and curly. Thoughtless adults coming into the home are in the habit of exclaiming over the beautiful hair of the younger child and only casually noticing the older girl. The mother realizes that the older girl is beginning to show evidences of jealousy and hostility toward the younger because of the attention she is getting. Very wisely, this mother watches for an opportunity when she is alone with the older girl to casually say something about the little sister's beautiful hair. "I'm sure you sometimes have wished that you had curly hair, too," says the mother. "I want you to know, though, that you ought to be very happy that your hair is straight. When you get older you can go to the beauty parlor and have your hair made curly, if that is the style; if the style calls for straight hair, you can have that, too."

Provide Successful Experiences

We should not minimize the part that failure plays in causing a child to lose confidence in himself. With enthusiasm and vigor he begins the task of overcoming the obstacles of life. Then he fails. He is face to face with the stark reality that not all of life is sunshine and success. Unless he is wisely guided, these failures may discourage further effort. It is the responsibility of every parent, therefore, to see to it that every child, without exception, has successful experiences and the exhilaration that accompanies merited expressions of approval. The new zest and self-confidence displayed by a young child who discovered that he could make solid-model airplanes as well as his older brother is a case in point. Inasmuch as boys and girls place a high estimate on athletic prowess, fathers should take time to help their children learn how to play ball, tennis, badminton, and the like. It takes a long time for a boy to get rid of the memory that he always was selected last whenever the gang chose up sides for a baseball game. If lack of muscular co-ordination makes even average athletic prowess impossible, other skills should be cultivated.

Important as are successful experiences for the development of self-confidence, the ability to face failure realistically and courageously is likewise important. The child who hasn't learned how to analyze his failures, get suggestions out of them for the future, and then forget those failures, is ill-equipped to face an adult life in which failures are certain to be mixed with accomplishments. Perhaps the most insecure and miserable of adults are those who are pathetically afraid of failure.

Take Children Seriously

When children or adolescents feel that adults are not taking them seriously, their self-confidence is undermined. Therefore never laugh at a child's remark unless it is meant to be funny. A four-year-old girl came to a class of adults who were considering the place of children in the Christian home. Sitting on the front row, the mother whispered to her that the leader of the class was going to preach. The child whispered so loudly that those around could hear, "I'm not going to let him preach." The leader, hearing this, smiled; others in the class smiled and laughed a bit; the child saw the amusement of the adults and with embarrassment hid her face in her hands, whimpered, and the mother felt it necessary to take her from the room. What a group of thoughtless adults! Of course the little girl was embarrassed; of course her confidence in the kindness and fairness of adults was shaken; of course her sense of security and feeling of self-confidence was lessened. The next time you are present when thoughtless adults burst out into laughter at a child's remark, look at the expression on the child's face; you will likely find evidences of dismay, hostility, and embarrassment. Remember, too, that teasing frequently produces the same result.

Give Approval

Self-confidence is much more likely to be the outcome of a moderate amount of praise than of excessive criticism. It is difficult to understand parents who seem to delight in criticizing their children. They apparently do not know, or have forgotten, that boys and girls as a rule are spurred on to greater effort by expressions of approval rather than by rebukes. At the same time it should be remembered that unmerited approval may make a child cynical of the judgment of adults, and give him a false outlook upon life.

Take Fears Seriously

If we are wise, we will take seriously the fears of our children, regardless of how ridiculous they may seem to be. We will do this because we realize that much of the misery and despair, not only of children but of young people and adults as well, may be traced to irrational and abnormal fears, fears that effectively interfere with the development of self-confidence. As we think of our own childhood and adolescence, we recall the agony of spirit caused by fears that now seem to us to be rather silly. But they weren't silly then. They were very real. And they are very real to boys and girls today.

Obviously we can't deal intelligently with the fears of childhood unless we recognize their presence. Sometimes children will tell us of them. Many times, however, they will not do so, either because they are ashamed of them, or because they find it difficult to express themselves. There are more or less unconscious fears, also, of which the child may be but dimly aware, but which nevertheless

64

influence his behavior and create in him a fearful attitude toward life.

Fear is frequently responsible for timidity and shyness. It usually is present when children lack a venturesome spirit and avoid all games or activities in which there is an element of danger. The fearful child has a tendency to withdraw from social groups and to take refuge in daydreaming. Unexplainable emotional upsets, especially during adolescence, may be due to unrecognized fears. Sometimes fear causes a child to become aggressive, loud, and boisterous. It may manifest itself in physical disorders for which there are no apparent reasons. For example, the six-year-old who had a sore throat every school morning was discovered to have a genuine fear of the school principal.

Fears Are Learned

There is rather widespread agreement that there are very few stimuli or situations that normally arouse the fear response. The withdrawal of support, loud noises, and sudden, violent, and strange stimuli seem to arouse fear in children. But there is no such thing, for example, as an instinctive fear of snakes, mice, or of anything slimy. These and other fears are learned, altogether too frequently from thoughtless adults. It is pretty well established that children are likely to have the fears of their parents. It is because most fears are learned that we can do something about them and guide our children so that they will not go out into life handicapped by them.

Here is an example of how certain fears are learned. A father bought for his baby a balloon that gave a loud squawk as the air came out of it. Instead of letting the child see and handle the balloon before it was blown up, he very foolishly blew it up and handed the squawking, strange object to the child. The child had never seen a balloon before, so instead of showing delight, as the father expected him to, he drew back and started crying. He was afraid. He was in the presence of something strange that produced a loud noise, the very stimuli that cause the fear response.

This general principle operates in the development of most fears of this type. A young child sees a puppy for the first time. The exuberant puppy rushes up to him, licks his face, and perhaps knocks him down. He develops a fear of dogs. Another child finds a harmless snake and plays with it. The frantic mother shouts at him to put it down, grabs him, and runs away from the snake. Thenceforth he

is afraid of snakes. Fear of the dark, of storms, and of all sorts of animals develops in this way.

Children are likely to fear anything that threatens their physical and emotional security. Because of their limited experience and lack of judgment they frequently reach false conclusions as to what is a real threat and suffer needlessly. Thoughtless remarks of parents and other adults contribute to these fears. A child hears his parent exaggerate the pain encountered in the dentist's chair or the doctor's office. He doesn't know it is an exaggeration, and develops a fear of dentists and doctors that remains throughout life. Sometimes a child hears the casual and half-laughing remark of his parent that they are headed for the poorhouse, takes it seriously, and until he is set aright is haunted by a depressing fear.

Some of the most pathetic fears of childhood and adolescence are those connected with the physical. A child, hearing an adult describe symptoms of a dread disease, may conclude that he has it. Adolescents, particularly, are sensitive concerning their bodies. They frequently wonder if their sexual development is normal, and may be distressed and embarrassed by the secondary physical changes that accompany puberty. If they have developed unfortunate habits, they are likely to worry and to have a deep sense of guilt. This sense of guilt in turns leads to a feeling of inferiority and a pessimistic attitude toward life.

Avoid Overstimulation

Exciting stories, movies, and television and radio programs are the source of many of the fears of childhood. The ten-year-old boy who, after an especially gruesome ghost story, had to have his window blinds pulled down each night and who begged to sleep in the same room with his parents is a case in point. The four- or five-year-old who almost went into hysterics whenever she passed a store window in which was a stuffed baboon had seen the awesome spectacle of Dr. Jekyll turning into Mr. Hyde in a movie a short time before. Although children need a moderate amount of excitement, parents should guard them from unusually exciting events or stories. To be sure, what is too exciting for one child may not be so for another. If, however, a child becomes irritable, restless, has difficulty sleeping at night, tosses unusually much in his sleep, or loses his appetite, it is likely he is having too much excitement during his waking hours.

Although there is no automatic fear-eliminating procedure, the following are suggestions usually given for helping children overcome fears that have developed:

1. *Find out the reason for the fear and remove it.* Fear of a disease, for example, may be eliminated by a physical examination that reveals the fear is groundless.

2. *Talk about the fears.* This helps to get them out into the open and may reduce their intensity in situations where they are not very great.

3. *Avoid the fear-producing stimulus.* Time frequently enables one to overcome fears that are not too intense.

4. *Provide distractions.* A mother and child were sitting at a window looking out at the brilliant flashes of lightning. A sudden crash of thunder frightened the mother, and she felt the child become tense. Quickly she controlled her own emotions and directed the attention of the child to the beauty of the sky. His attention thus was diverted before the fear response began to operate.

5. *Encourage social imitation.* A small child was afraid of elevators. Two larger children whom he greatly admired went with him on a visit to a hospital. They did not know of his fear, so took him by the hand and without any

68

question walked into the elevator. The child went willingly and exhibited no fear.

6. *Help the child associate happy experiences with that which is feared.* A small child was afraid of doctors. The new doctor, however, always took the child's hand and drew interesting pictures on the back of it with his pen. Soon the child looked forward to his visits. It is this process of reconditioning that is perhaps the most effective method of overcoming fears.

A final word. Our discussion has centered about unwholesome fears. A moderate amount of fear is wholesome. Fearlessness is closely associated with recklessness. We don't want our children to be afraid of snakes, for example, but we do want them to have a healthy fear of poisonous ones and to be able to recognize them. When a child crosses the street, a healthy fear makes him more alert and watchful. But in helping children develop wholesome fears, we need to guard against being overapprehensive and constantly reminding them of dangers.

CHAPTER 6

Social Adjustment and Discipline

*L*ET'S LISTEN TO SOME PARENTS TALKING. FIRST OF all, a mother of a child of three is saying, "What can I do to help my child get along better with her playmates? She is so selfish. She likes children of her own age but can't get along with them."

Then there are the parents of a ten-year-old boy. They are saying, "Somewhere in our guidance of Tom we must have failed. He is so timid and shy when guests are present that it is embarrassing both to him and to them. Perhaps we should have had more guests in the home when he was younger."

The mother of a fifteen-year-old boy addresses a friend, "I wish I knew how to get Harry out with young people more. He spends all of his time studying or reading, and seems to have no desire to go to parties or have dates or even to have many friends."

Social Adjustment Is Important

These parents are quite properly concerned about the social adjustment of their children. Boys and girls who do not get along well with people are likely to have a sense of frustration and to be filled with inhibitions that keep them from adjusting well in other areas of life. A study of junior high school students shows that those who do not get along well with their fellows not only are unhappy personally, but are unable to concentrate well and consequently do poorly in their studies.

Companions and friends help one to become emotionally mature. Their appreciation adds to the joy of success, their confidence spurs one on to greater efforts, and their understanding lessens the agony of sorrow and dulls the biting edge of failure. Furthermore, the ability to get along with others may spell the difference between vocational success and failure. Think of your own friends who have achieved places of distinction in their work. Has not their personality, as well as their ability, been responsible for their success?

Respect Individual Differences

It is well to remind ourselves that some children are temperamentally more inclined to be sociable than are others. Our task as parents is not to defy these temperamental differences or to insist that all children develop the same pattern of sociability. Let us rejoice in the child whose interest in school is in extracurricular activities, and who is popular with his classmates; but let us also help him develop good study habits. Let us rejoice equally in the child whose intellectual interests make of his studies a fascinating adventure and leave him little time for outside activities; but then let us encourage him to develop social graces and skills so that he will find satisfaction in the company of his fellows. What we are concerned about is not that all children shall be "social butterflies" or "good mixers," but that they shall like people and be able to get along well with them.

Sociability Is Learned

The significant point for parents to remember is that a child must learn how to get along with his fellows. He must be taught to be kind to other children, to be tolerant of their interests, and to be willing to share with them that which he has. He must develop skills and social graces that cause people to like him as a person and that make him an acceptable member of a group.

As parents guide the social development of their boys and girls, the following principles should be kept in mind.

1. *Do not expect a higher type of social behavior than is normal for the age of your child.* A small child is self-centered and, according to adult standards, selfish. The three-year-old mentioned at the beginning of this chapter was quite normal in her desire to keep for herself her toys. Children of this age, although happy to be with other children, tend to play by themselves. There is very little co-operative activity among them. When they are together, there should be sufficient toys on hand for everyone. An alert teacher or parent will note when two children are about to demand the same toy, and, by diverting the attention of one to another toy or activity, will avoid a conflict situation. Children rather early catch the idea of taking turns. They should not be reprimanded when they are slow to do so, as such reproof may cause them to develop a very undesirable sense of guilt and emotional insecurity. Praise and appreciation, however, should be given to those who do co-operate and share.

Growing boys and girls increasingly become co-operative in their relationships with each other. They discover that if they are going to get along with others they must relinquish some of their rights. There will continue to be the inevitable clash of wills—the quarrels and fights and temporary disagreements—but through it all there will be an increasing appreciation and regard for the rights of others.

2. *Make certain that children have an opportunity to play with other children.* It is through play that children

72

learn sociability. If parents have only one child, they should make every possible effort to get him into groups of children of his own age. The give-and-take of play is an indispensable experience for boys and girls. Let us invite children into our own yards and homes, remembering always that happy, adjusted children are far more important than a lawn of velvet or a house that is always in spick-and-span order. A camping experience in the summer with other boys and girls develops skill in adjusting to others.

In order that children may feel at ease with children of all ages, they should have contacts with those who are older than they are. It is unfortunate, however, when most of a child's friends are not of his own age.

3. *The example of parents is an important factor in the teaching of consideration for others.* This applies not only to their relationships with outsiders but to those in the family as well. If parents speak sharply to their children, forget the little courtesies such as the "thank you," and interrupt them when they are speaking, they do not have a right to expect other than the same kind of behavior from them.

4. *Have guests frequently in the home.* Wise parents let children help plan for the entertainment of guests. Suggestions may be made as to how they should be greeted and what may be done to make them feel at ease. It is helpful to give children an idea of what to talk about with the guests. It may be that the guest will be interested in the child's collection. The child in turn may be eager to hear about some of the interesting experiences of the guest.

Although children should have the experience of entertaining guests, they also need to realize that they must not monopolize the situation and cannot always be the center

73

of attention. After children have greeted the guests and have been with them for a while, they may then be excused to go out to play.

5. *Help children develop skills that will make them acceptable to groups.* It is difficult to overemphasize the importance of this. If boys and girls are to "rate" with their companions, they must have some skills and abilities. These may be in athletics, in music, dramatics, journalism, in scholarship, in the making of airplane models, or in any other activity that is popular with the group.

6. *Help boys and girls to be personally attractive.* One of the primary concerns of boys and girls, adolescents especially, is that they shall be popular, and it contributes considerably to their poise and self-assurance if they feel that their clothes and, in the case of girls, their facial make-up pass the test of their peers. Parents will keep up with the styles of the day and will let their daughters and sons select clothes that are worn "by the gang." To feel under or overdressed is an embarrassing experience that leads to a sense of inferiority.

The father has a responsibility to his daughter in this matter of giving her assurance as to her personal attractiveness. She is sensitive about her appearance and fears that boys will not find her attractive. If he compliments her about her dresses, complexion, and the way she wears her hair, she will have far more self-assurance when she gets into a group than if her father ignores her.

7. *Help boys and girls maintain their status with their group.* The skills mentioned above, as well as personal attractiveness, give boys and girls status with their fellows. Manners, too, are important. Such simple problems as how to introduce people, what to talk about, how to excuse oneself, who does the ordering at the drugstore or res-

taurant, are important to one who is trying to make a good impression.

Understanding parents will try to find out what it is that is disturbing their boys and girls and that makes them feel as though they are losing status with their fellows. It may be that they have to come in at night before the rest of the gang does. They may not have as much spending money as they think they should have. A girl may be embarrassed by her mother's being "too nice" to eligible young men. A boy may feel his father is silly when he tries to be a "good sport" when with high-school boys and girls. Children are sensitive concerning their parent's use of authority when their friends are around. A ten-year-old rushed breathlessly into the house one evening upon the call of his father and said, "Dad, whenever you want to talk to me or tell me to do something, call me in and be sure not to come out where the other boys are."

Whatever it is that disturbs boys and girls, let us talk about it and see what solution can be reached. We may need to make certain compromises on relatively unimportant matters, and in some cases lighten restrictions. When they face problems caused by different standards and ideals, we need to help them see how they can maintain their own self-respect without being a "wet blanket" to those who disagree with them. The solution of these problems is made much easier if we are willing to let our homes become social centers for the activities of boys and girls.

Discipline in the Home

"To spank or not to spank, that is the question." That the question of spanking is of vital interest to parents can be attested to by anyone who has met with any considerable number of parents' groups. They are interested in finding out if physical punishment is ever justifiable. Nevertheless, the more fundamental question is this: How can we help children choose for themselves that kind of behavior that is personally satisfying and socially acceptable? A consideration of this question gets us into the whole problem of authority and freedom in the home, obedience and methods of discipline.

It was suggested in the first chapter that although a Christian home will be run on democratic principles, democracy does not mean the complete absence of authority. Authority will not be used for its own sake, however, and therefore will be used sparingly. It will always be thought of in terms of what its use will mean to the growth and development of the children in the home.

Unfortunately, parents who feel insecure themselves and who are finding life disappointing and thwarting are rarely able to exercise wisely the authority that is theirs by virtue of their parenthood. On the one hand, they are likely to exercise authority over the children primarily as a means of bolstering their own faltering ego, and to use methods that will impose their will upon them rather than will create in them a desire for more desirable behavior. Such parents are emotionally immature. They control their children by fear rather than by love or reason. To all outward appearances it seems at times as though they get excellent results. Their children obey promptly, never talk back, and do the tasks assigned to them without quibbling. What is not so apparent is the inner resentment toward the parents that the children are acquiring, the lack of experience and skill in making their own decisions, the stifling of initiative and resourcefulness, and the development of an attitude either of rebellion or meek acquiescence toward all authority.

On the other hand, parents who feel insecure may be

afraid to use their authority for fear it will endanger the love and respect of their children for them. Mothers or fathers who are not happy in their own relationships to each other may bestow upon one or more of the children the love they should reserve for each other. They become so dependent upon the good will of their children for their own sense of security that they do nothing to interfere with the whims and desires of the children. They thoroughly spoil them. Consequently the children become self-centered, inconsiderate of and unable to get along with others, and lack the self-discipline that is so essential for proper adjustment to life. Such children go out into the world ill prepared to take their place in it.

Parents who are emotionally mature will neither magnify nor minimize the authority they possess. They will not be afraid to say "No" to their children when they deem it necessary, but neither will they be afraid to change their minds if they find they have thoughtlessly and without a good reason answered a child's request in the negative. They will give their children as much freedom as their age and experience enable them to use constructively. They will encourage the growth of the spirit of independence, at the same time that they are trying to create in the members of the family a spirit of co-operation and consideration for each other. They will deal with each situation in the light of all the factors in that situation, rather than by any stereotyped procedure.

It should be remembered that children themselves welcome authority when it is wisely administered. They may grumble at the restrictions and decisions of parents at times, but underneath there is a sense of security in the realization that their parents will protect them from danger and will keep them from doing that which may have disastrous results.

Two questions of concern to many parents are these: (1) How can I get my children to obey? (2) What method of discipline shall I use when they do not obey or when their behavior seems to call for discipline?

Securing Obedience

It is essential that children shall learn to respect authority and to abide by the rules of the family and of society. Nevertheless, it is possible for children to be too obedient. A child who always obeys without any question is likely to lack that initiative, resourcefulness, and independence of spirit that we want our children to have. I suspect, however, that most of you are not faced with the problem of a child that is too obedient. Here are some suggestions, therefore, that may be helpful as you seek to secure obedience from your children:

1. *Do not give commands that call for obedience unless you are certain they are necessary.* Many parents thoughtlessly shower their children with "do's" and "don'ts" from morning until night. A multitude of commands which even the parents do not expect the children to take too seriously, soon create in the children the feeling that their parents' directions are not too important. As parents limit their commands to situations that are really important and see to it that they are carried out, the habit of obedience is much more likely to be learned.

2. *Whenever possible, which will be most of the time, give reasons for your commands.* If children discover that you don't "give orders" without a good reason, they are more likely to respond favorably when reasons cannot be given.

3. *Guard against the tone of voice used in issuing commands.* A "Now you've got to do this, Son, whether you want to or not" attitude is likely to create resentment

and perhaps rebellion in a self-respecting youngster who is striving for independence. Insofar as possible use requests and suggestions rather than commands.

4. *Give children time to "get ready" to obey.* For example, let children know that in five or ten minutes you expect them to be ready to come to dinner or go to bed. This gives them an opportunity to finish what they are doing.

5. *Children sometimes respond more readily and happily to an impersonal signal than they do to the spoken word.* The parents of one family found that a "toot-toot" on the car horn brought quick response from their children. A policeman's whistle is sometimes effective.

6. *If children who usually obey fairly well suddenly become exceedingly disobedient, look for the reason in some emotional disturbance.* Such a child may not be getting along well with other children; he may have been disappointed at school or be failing in his classwork; he may be disturbed because of a sense of guilt due to hostility feelings or unfortunate physical habits he may have acquired. Your clue is to try to help overcome the situation that is causing the emotional upset.

7. *Expect your children to be obedient.* Don't give them the impression that you know they will disobey, and that they will be punished for their disobedience. But do not expect perfection from them, either with respect to obedience or in any other way. Sometimes disobedience is the result of your not having taken the time to make your wishes clearly known. Remember that a child who is called from some interesting activity to "get orders" from you may appear to be listening to what you have to say, but in reality his thoughts are somewhere else. Sometimes, too, children just forget. Don't we all!

Methods of Discipline

Insofar as methods of discipline are concerned, it is exceedingly important that parents should think of discipline not so much in terms of punishment as in terms of guidance. To think of discipline primarily as punishment is likely to develop in the parents a "punishment psychology," and the feeling that their responsibility is primarily that of meting out punishment and rewards. They should not think of themselves as "policemen."

The secret of successful discipline—and this is important —lies not so much in any one method as in the feeling of rapport that exists between parents and children—the presence of genuine love, affection, and understanding. When such a relationship exists between parents and children, even faulty methods of discipline may not have disastrous results. At the same time it would be a mistake to assume that the method of discipline is of no importance. Wrong methods sometimes make impossible the rapport just mentioned.

It should be remembered, furthermore, that it is impossible to give a stereotyped list of successful methods of discipline. Remember the discussion on individual differences? A method that may be successfully used by one parent with a particular child may be quite unsatisfactory when used by another parent either with the same child or another. Each parent, therefore, will seek to discover— sometimes through the trial and error method—the procedure that seems for him to be the most effective in guiding his children. It is to be hoped that the parent will think of himself as a guide rather than as a disciplinarian. Such an approach makes much easier the development of a wholesome relationship with children.

Granting that successful discipline is largely an individual matter, there are some general principles that may well be kept in mind.

1. *Insofar as possible the method of discipline should arise naturally out of the behavior.* A child who through carelessness or destructiveness finds himself without his skates should be expected to get along without them, at least for sufficient time so that he recognizes the logical outcome of such behavior. Children who will not play

together without an unusual amount of bickering and fighting should be isolated from each other for a long enough time to realize that antisocial behavior isolates one from his fellows.

This approach to discipline means that many times the results of the behavior are all the discipline that the child needs. A four-year-old, for example, bouncing a tennis ball in the house, bounced it so high it knocked off a lovely vase from the bookshelf. It was a vase that the boy loved and admired. He was heartbroken, and his own regret for what he had done was sufficient discipline.

On the other hand it may be that the logical outcome of a child's behavior will be more disastrous than the child should be expected to bear. Mrs. Sidonie Gruenberg gives as an example of this a child losing an overcoat at the beginning of the winter season. Obviously a child can't go through the winter without an overcoat, and the parents will need to get him another. Mrs. Gruenberg then adds a comment that the home should be a place where children are able to learn from their mistakes rather than to suffer because of them. Let's not forget that.

2. *Methods of discipline that have no logical relationship to the behavior itself—spanking, withdrawal of special privileges, certain types of isolation, scolding, and the like—although at times understandable if not permissible, should always be recognized as having temporary value only and as having limited value in directing children into desirable ways of behaving.*

A word should be said, however, about spanking inasmuch as this method is so widely used and is of considerable concern to parents. There are those who feel that for very young children a slap on the hand or an occasional spanking may not be harmful, indeed, at times may even be helpful. Whether spanking should be used even then, however, depends upon the reaction of the child to it, and the particular situation. A two-year-old boy who developed the habit of biting other children when things did not go his way was helped by spanking, because the father had impressed upon him the fact that biting would always be followed by spanking. Even in this case, however, a more intelligent method might have been devised.

The danger of any form of physical punishment arises primarily out of the fact that it is so much easier to spank than to make the effort to discover more intelligent ways of discipline. Spanking not only is the easiest, but is usually the least intelligent form of discipline. Even a moron can spank! Obviously a parent should not spank when angry, or until alternative methods of discipline have been considered. It should be remembered, too, that the peak of the spanking age is approximately three, and that as children get older this method becomes decreasingly effective.

3. *When it seems necessary to use a disciplinary method, let it be used immediately.* Guard against postponing discipline until Father gets home, for example. Also, do not threaten the use of discipline at some later time.

CHAPTER 7

Some Perennial Problems

I N THIS CHAPTER WE SHALL CONSIDER SOME OF THE perennial problems that parents face as they endeavor to guide wisely their growing children.

Sex Education

Those who are concerned about the emotional and spiritual health of their children will rejoice in the high privilege that is theirs in helping them develop wholesome attitudes toward sex and the miracle of propagation. They will realize that it is natural and right for boys and girls to be curious about sex and that it is the parents' place to supply the desired information. If they do not do so, the information will be secured elsewhere and probably in such a way as to create undesirable attitudes toward the whole subject. Mistaken information and wrong ideas about sex may cause children to worry, to have feelings of guilt and shame, and may make it difficult in later life to have wholesome and normal relationships with those of the opposite sex. The parents' obligation, therefore, is to provide a sane program of sex education in the home, an obligation they dare not neglect.

Many parents will find that their first problem in such a program is with themselves. Intellectually they have overcome their own childish ideas that nice people don't talk about sex and that any interest in the subject isn't quite right; emotionally, however, they have not done so. Consequently when their children ask questions in this area, they tend to get embarrassed; they blush, and their voices become tense as they endeavor to answer them. Such behavior on their part is likely to give children the impression that sex is either very mysterious, or bad, or both. The first task of the parent, therefore, is to get himself to the place where he can discuss sex naturally and calmly.

In helping children develop wholesome attitudes toward sex, the following should be kept in mind:

1. *Sex education begins during the first few years of life as children begin to notice and ask questions about the various parts of their own bodies, or about the bodies of their parents, brothers, or sisters.* These questions should be answered calmly and frankly, and the correct names for the various parts and functions of the body should be given. Boys and girls during these early years should be given their baths together, and undue emphasis should not be placed upon modesty lest they reach the conclusion that there is something shameful about the human body.

2. *Questions about sex do not require an extended discussion of the subject.* Answer only the question asked by the child; do not elaborate on it.

3. *If one is to be ready to answer questions, he should anticipate some of the questions that are certain to be asked.* One can be certain, for example, that there will come a time when a child will want to know where babies come from. If one is not prepared to answer this question, he may show confusion and give an answer which he later will have difficulty explaining to the child. One mother, for example, told her small son that babies came from tigers. Two years later she reported that he still thought babies came from tigers, and she wanted to know how she should give him the correct information!

There are many pamphlets and books available that

will help parents know how to answer the specific questions children ask about sex. Some of these are listed in the Suggestions for Further Reading.

4. *Cats or dogs in the home that give birth to their young provide excellent opportunities for sex education.*

5. *The arrival of a new baby in the home or in a neighboring home should be utilized to talk about the miracle of birth.* Children who are informed of the coming of a new baby brother or sister and who are told something about the baby's development within the mother not only get desirable information but likewise develop a protective attitude toward both the mother and the babe-to-be. The whole story of propagation, including the father's part, if the child asks questions about it, is thus associated with a joyful family experience. A child with this background is fortified against any attempt of less fortunate companions to make something vulgar and shameful of sex and the process of birth.

6. *Boys are not turned over to fathers and girls to mothers for their sex instruction.* The parent who gets the question should answer it.

7. *Sex teaching should be as casual as possible and not limited to special periods.* Sex should be treated as simply one of the many phases of life, and its importance should not be unduly stressed.

8. *Adolescents are likely to be rather reticent about discussing sex matters with their parents.* It is important, however, that they know something about the changes that are taking place in their own bodies. Parents will try to arrange for situations in which it will seem natural and proper to talk about these matters. If it is impossible to do so, and if adolescents do not ask any questions, it will be well to have helpful pamphlets and books on sex develop-

ment about the house where they may readily be found. *Growing Up*, by De Schweinitz, is helpful for pre-adolescent children. *Being Born*, by Strain, is excellent for those of junior high school age and even a bit younger. *Life and Growth*, by Keliher, and *Facts of Life and Love for Teenagers*, by Duvall, answer the questions of high-school boys and girls. Pamphlets that are interesting and helpful to boys and girls are listed in the Suggestions for Further Reading.

There are some excellent films on human reproduction that may be secured for showing either in the public schools or in the church. Parents should encourage their public school administrators and church leaders to show them.

9. *Boys and girls should be told about the organs and the process of reproduction in the other sex as well as their own.*

10. *Small children need not be told about sex crimes, prostitution, or venereal disease.* Older boys and girls and adolescents, however, have only to turn to the latest newspaper to read about them. Be ready, therefore, to talk to them about the fact that there are those who misuse the sex power that God expects us to express within the marriage relationship.

It is during adolescence that boys and girls begin to notice each other with new interest and appreciation. Wise parents will recognize this as wholesome and natural, and will encourage their children to have many friends of the opposite sex. It should be remembered that sex interest is likely to be much more abnormal and unwholesome when boys and girls are separated than when they have normal contacts with each other.

Now is the time, too, when boys and girls will profit from hearing about the early love affairs of their parents, their standards with respect to sex, and something of the joy that comes from entering the marriage relationship with a clean body and a clear conscience.

This is the time, also, when the question of petting becomes a real problem to many boys and girls. If they approach their parents about the problem, they should be heard sympathetically and understandingly. It should be granted that the desire to give some physical expression of one's affection is normal. At the same time they may be helped to see all that is involved in petting—the tendency it has to magnify the importance of physical thrills and to minimize other mutual interests, how promiscuous petting cheapens one's sense of values and how it may lead to loss of self-control and behavior that one will forever after regret. Let there be no preaching nor condemnation, but simply a sincere desire to help them meet squarely and sanely a real problem.

The pamphlet *Petting—Wise or Otherwise,* by Clarke, will be helpful to young people facing this problem. Excellent help also may be found in Burkhart's *From Friendship to Marriage;* Elliott and Bone's *The Sex Life of Youth;* Strain's *Love at the Threshold;* and Duvall's *Facts of Life and Love for Teenagers.*

It has been noted that many who pet unwisely do so because of a sense of insecurity and the feeling that their parents neither care for nor have confidence in them. Therefore one way to help our boys and girls in this matter of petting is to assure them of our own love and affection and of our confidence in their integrity. We should also help them develop a variety of interests and skills so that they need not depend upon petting for popularity.

Let us remind ourselves again of the important part that the atmosphere of the home and its ideals play upon boys and girls. If the parents love each other and do not hesitate to show it, if the family ideals are high, and if there is a sense of comradeship and fellowship among the members of the family, boys and girls are likely to develop wholesome attitudes toward sex.

The Family and Its Money

It would be interesting and perhaps revealing to note how frequently money enters into the family conversation and how many times it is responsible for family problems and worries. It is of value, therefore, to face frankly and realistically ways by which money may be made to contribute to, rather than interfere with, wholesome family living.

The following may be thought of as prerequisites for the successful handling of money by the family:

1. *A wholesome relationship among members of the family*. If members of the family have genuine affection for and confidence in one another, if the spirit of unselfishness, tolerance, and respect governs their relationships, and if self-control is practiced, successful solutions of money problems will be found. We are likely to manage money with the same success that we manage all the other relationships of life. If we are careless in our work and personal habits, we are likely to be careless with money. If we lack personal discipline and self-control, we will find it difficult to spend money wisely. Management of money, therefore, is but one phase of learning how to manage one's life.

2. *A wholesome attitude toward money—an attitude which leads one neither to overestimate nor to minimize its importance*. This attitude grows out of the realization that money is simply a means by which one may achieve some of the great values of life. When money itself becomes a value, its main function is forgotten, other values are minimized, and life becomes a mad pursuit for the "al-

mighty dollar." If the main topic of conversation in the home is money, if there is an attitude of subservience and envy toward those of wealth, children inevitably reach the conclusion that acquisition of money is the main purpose of life. Leland Foster Wood, in commenting on the statement of Jesus, "Ye cannot serve God and mammon," suggests that he might have said, "You cannot be preoccupied with money and have a rich home atmosphere."

But let us not underestimate the importance of money and of learning how to handle it wisely. In our present economy a certain amount of money is essential for the needs of life. We want our boys and girls to reach maturity with a real appreciation of the value of money, the ability to make a decent living, the knowledge of how to spend constructively and save wisely, and the desire to give generously to worthy causes. These goals will not be reached without careful planning by the parents.

3. *A determination to live within one's income.* Nothing can bring a greater sense of frustration to members of the family, even the children, than the realization that the outgo is exceeding the income. As debts pile up, nerves become frayed and tempers quick. It becomes easy to accuse one another of recklessness in spending, of selfishness, and of indifference to the family welfare. The father is likely to feel his efforts are not appreciated. His resentment is accompanied by a feeling of inferiority. Confidence in one another is supplanted by suspicion, affection by irritation. Family pride gives way to the fear of family disgrace. Wood makes the thought-provoking comment that "there are many families which by cutting their expenditures ten or twenty per cent could increase their family happiness one hundred per cent."

It is important to realize that whereas we should give our children the best we can afford, it is no kindness to them to give them *more* than we can afford! We prepare our children best for life when we teach them to live within our income.

4. *Desires that can be satisfied with a minimum expenditure of money.* Fortunate is the family whose members have many desires that can be satisfied with a minimum expenditure of money. It costs relatively little—perhaps only the cost of carfare—to enjoy the beauties of a park or a hike through the woods. The joy of digging in fresh dirt, of planting seeds and watching them grow, is ours for a small cost. The family night at home: playing games, singing, relating interesting experiences, or working on hobbies—costs little in terms of money. Inspiring and informing books give zest to life and can be secured for a few cents from the public library. We impoverish the lives of our children if we fail to create in them a desire for values that can be realized with little financial cost.

5. *Democracy in the expenditure of the family income.* Each member of the family, with the exception of small children, should be aware of the amount of the family income and have something to say about how it will be spent. Gone are the days when it was considered proper for the husband to keep his family in ignorance concerning his financial status, and to dole out with a great show of munificence a few dollars to the wife and a few cents to the children.

A Budget Has Value

It should be remembered that careful planning is much more likely to lead to the wise use of the family income than is spending on the impulse of the moment. Hence the importance of a budget. Without a budget many families would soon be spending more than comes in. A budget encourages prompt payment of bills and thus helps to keep the family credit good. If it is intelligently and democratically determined, it tends to create in each member of the family a co-operative spirit so far as the expenditure of the

income is concerned. Children who have had a share in making the budget and who know what has been allotted to them to spend are much less likely to tease for additional sums than those who feel that what they get is largely the result of the parents' whim of the moment. Neither are

92

they so likely to feel resentful when they cannot have everything they want. As Elizabeth Reisner has said, there is a world of difference between saying, "I can't afford it," and "Let us see if we can afford it," when children come with requests involving the expenditure of money.

In making the budget let each member of the family list his or her needs and wants. Do not forget that future as well as immediate needs should be listed. Classify these needs under some such general headings as: (1) material needs, (2) cultural, recreational, and aesthetic needs, (3) giving, and (4) saving. It is then necessary to decide how much of the family income will be devoted to each classification. Although no two families will make a similar decision, the following possible distribution of the income suggested by Florence Barnard may be helpful: savings, 20 per cent; giving, 10 per cent; necessities, 50 per cent; betterments, 20 per cent.

It is exceedingly important that the budget should include a sum to meet any emergencies that not only may but are certain to arise. Let this emergency fund be cumulative. Each member of the family, of course, will be given the responsibility of spending a certain proportion of the income, the amount depending upon his maturity, needs, and responsibilities. A record or an account will be kept, but it should not be permitted to become a burden. There will be no attempt to make the budget balance to the last penny, although a fair degree of accuracy in accounting is essential of course. The budget will always be thought of as a servant, not as a master. Its purpose is not to take the joy out of life, but rather to add joy to it.

Allowances

Each child should have an allowance when he begins to feel the need for money. Some children will feel this need much earlier than others, as early as five or six. The amount of the allowance will depend upon what the child is expected to purchase with it and upon how much allowance his friends receive. The amount will be increased as the child grows and as his needs and ability to spend money increase. Una Bernard Sait reminds us that an excellent principle to keep in mind is that a child's financial resources should never be so great that it is unnecessary for him to consider relative values, "nor so small as to make choice and planning impossible."

The educational values of the allowance are realized only as it really belongs to the child and its expenditure is exclusively under his control. For example, when we give a child fifteen cents as an allowance and tell him that he must save five cents and give five cents to the church, his real allowance is the five cents that he has to spend as he wishes.

Although a child should be permitted to make his own decision as to how to spend his allowance, he should receive some guidance from his parents. Their task is to provide him with experiences in which he finds out the value of money, the regret accompanying the unwise use of it, and the satisfaction that follows wise expenditures. The first time a child is taken to a "ten-cent store" with some money of his own, he is likely to purchase the first toy that he sees. The parents may suggest, but should not insist, that he postpone the purchase until he has looked around. It is an excellent experience for him to buy this toy, however, and then discover upon further search that there is another toy he would much rather have. The parents can spoil the value of the experience, of course, if, feeling sorry for him, they purchase this second toy for him. It is by trial and error that boys and girls learn how to spend discriminatingly and to realize the value of money.

For the adolescent an adequate allowance is essential for his own self-respect and emotional security. By the time a child is fourteen he should be able to manage a rather comprehensive allowance that covers such items as clothing, amusements, carfare, Scout dues, contributions to church and charity, and other necessary expenditures. If school lunches are included in the allowance, parents will be wise to check up occasionally to make sure the child is not stinting on them in order to have money for something he desires more.

An enriching and educational experience for every member of the family is that which accompanies the conference that should precede the decision to make a major expenditure of the family income, whether it be for a home, a car, the sending of the children to a summer camp, or for a family trip. These questions will be asked: What will the contemplated expenditure do to the family budget? Will it necessitate cutting down here and there, and if so, is it worth it? What can each member of the family do to make the expenditure possible? As boys and girls share in such discussions, they develop a sense of loyalty to and responsibility for the successful ongoing of the family.

Giving and Saving

In teaching children to give we should keep in mind the following:

1. *The example of the parents is tremendously important—not only what they give, but the spirit with which they give.*

2. *Children should be provided with experiences in which genuine satisfaction comes from giving.* For example, a small child who was somewhat timid and who seldom indicated a desire to give to others was encouraged

to take some popcorn balls to his friends at Christmas-time. His first reaction was to refuse, but he finally took some to the door of a friend. As he came back to the car, his eyes were shining and he said with considerable enthusiasm, "That's fun." Children need to find out that there is joy in giving.

3. *A desire to give is created when children have specific information as to the use that will be made of their gifts.* As they are made aware—either through pictures, stories, or visits—of the fact that other boys and girls need toys, food, or clothing, they feel impelled to help provide them with gifts. Giving to a cause "in general" is not likely to be especially satisfying or to create a continuing desire to give. It is for this reason that it is important that they should be given information as to how the money is expended that they give to the church and the church school.

4. *As children get older and have an allowance, their gifts should be their own and should not represent "something given to them by their parents to give."* By the time they are ten or twelve, and in some cases earlier, they should have been made acquainted with the ways in which the church uses the money that is given to it. They are now ready to make a pledge to the church, to receive envelopes, and to make their contribution weekly. This not only instills within them the habit of systematic giving, but makes them feel that they really belong to the church.

5. *Families are wise if they plan for "giving projects" of their own in which each member of the family participates.* At the family council assignments may be made to various members of the family for finding out the needs of boys and girls and families in their community, and, indeed, throughout the world. After reporting their find-

ings to the council, they can make a decision as to what the family giving project should be and how each member of the family may contribute to it. For example, should the decision be to help a family in Europe that does not have enough to eat, it may be decided to have a sacrificial meal each week, the money saved by such a meal to be used to send a CARE package. If it is decided to send clothes, children should be encouraged to send not only their old clothing but an article of clothing that they prize as well. The family as a group, as well as individuals, can discover that "giving is fun."

Saving, too, is important. Small children, of course, will not save for an indefinite future. But they can begin to realize that if they want something in the store that costs more than they now have on hand, they can get it next week if they will save their allowance this week. A nine-year-old boy wanted to buy an unusually good baseball glove. For several weeks, therefore, he saved out of his allowance. When he had a sufficient sum, he began to shop—with the money in his pocket—and found just the glove he wanted. It was a most satisfying experience. As boys and girls get into their teens, they will have sensed the value of putting aside some of their allowance for rather remote needs; saving has become a policy.

A word of warning to parents is in order, however. Your child may spend his allowance for the week the first day or so after he receives it. Out of pity in your heart you may be tempted to advance him something out of the following week's allowance. If you start this, you will find it brings you considerable trouble. Furthermore, it gets the child into the habit of running into debt and of living beyond his income, a habit that may persist as an adult. Obviously it discourages saving.

Children Sharing in the Work of the Home

As members of the family group children have a right to an allowance. Also, as members of the family group, children should be expected to share in the responsibilities of the home. Furthermore, it is only as children help in the work of the home that they develop a sense of responsibility and discover the joy of co-operative effort. Initiative, independence of spirit, a sense of their own worth, and a willingness to submerge personal interests in the larger interests of the family develop in the child who has learned to carry cheerfully and well his share of the many tasks that abound in the modern home. A parent robs a child when he deprives him of the opportunity to achieve these values. The child who has been waited upon hand and foot has difficulty adjusting himself to life outside of the home. The most effective way to make our children parasites in society is to permit them to be parasites in the home.

The question that concerns most of us, however, is not whether our children should help with the household duties, but rather how to get them to help. And by this we do not mean grudging help that is accompanied by moans and groans and an air of martyrdom. That isn't what we want. We want their cheerful co-operation. If we can't get it and if we find we have to keep after them about their chores, we soon give up and prefer to do the work ourselves rather than to be irritated constantly by a forgetful child. But that's where we make our mistake. Children cannot always be expected to enjoy their work or never to forget. Furthermore, they do not develop responsibility except as we patiently direct and guide them. This getting children to help in the home is a skill that we need to acquire. Here are some suggestions that may be helpful.

1. *Begin early.* Many parents continue to wait upon a

child long after he is able to wait upon himself. Encourage your small child to dress himself, wash his hands and face, and to pick up his toys. Find other simple tasks that he can do, such as bringing in the milk, dusting, or setting the table. Remember, however, that he will not do these as well as you would. If you are more concerned about a scrubbed and shining face or dustless chairs than you are about the development of initiative and a sense of responsibility, you will continue to spoil your child. This does not mean, of course, that you will encourage him to do shoddy work.

2. *Let him have a part in deciding what his duties shall be.* Have a family council in which a list of the home responsibilities are drawn up—things that must be done each day and each week in order to keep the home running smoothly and efficiently. After some discussion let each member of the family make a check by the responsibilities he is willing to assume. The children may not make many checks, but begin with those that they do make.

3. *Let the assignments be very specific, both as to the duties themselves and as to the time when they are to be performed.* Don't expect a child just to "stand by" in order to be helpful. Let the duties be simple and definite so that he will know when he has finished them. If he knows when they must be done, he can plan his play and other activities accordingly.

4. *The duties should not require a great deal of time.* The main responsibility of children is to attend school and do well there. They also need plenty of time for play.

5. *Sometimes children work better with others.* A father reports that his daughter who would work only ten or fifteen minutes at a time alone in the garden would work an hour or more when he was working with her.

6. It frequently is helpful to have a bulletin board on which are noted each day the responsibilities of each member of the family. This bulletin board serves as an impersonal reminder of one's duties, and it can be fun checking them off as they are completed. Although it may be necessary occasionally to remind children of their duties, guard against nagging about them.

7. See to it that responsibilities are changed frequently, perhaps every week or month. Some home duties are much more of a burden than others, and it is hardly fair to expect one member of the family to have the unpleasant tasks all the time.

8. Be sure their responsibilities are those that they can do well so their performance will give them the satisfaction that comes from something well done. Their tasks should be significant ones that make a real contribution to the smooth running of the household. "Made" work will not do.

9. Remember that example, especially that of the dad, is very important. Every member of the family, therefore, should participate in the work of the home.

10. Have good times together as a family. It is as members of a family enjoy, understand, and respect one another that the spirit of co-operation develops. Play is a great developer of understanding and fellowship. When members of the family play together, they are much more likely to work happily together.

Dealing with Falsehoods

If we discover that our children are not always telling the truth, let us not get upset but make a serious effort to discover why they find it easier to lie. Sometimes parents themselves without realizing it are largely responsible for their children's falsehoods. We need to ask ourselves these questions: Are we expecting too much of them in their schoolwork, in their ability to get along with their playmates, or in their ability to exercise self-control? Do we speak sharply to them and scold them when they displease us? How frequently do we punish them? If we neither scold nor punish, do we assume an injured air when they do not come up to our expectations? In other words, is it really easier for them if we do not know all the facts? If so, is it really surprising that they should be tempted to fib occasionally?

On the other hand, falsehoods may be a method of compensating for a feeling of weakness and insecurity. If children are not doing well in school and are not being accepted by their playmates, they may lie in order to secure what they think will be our approval. They want others to think well of them so they tell of possessions and achievements that have reality only in their dreams.

If the answers to the above questions give some insight into the reasons for our children's falsehoods, the cure will consist largely in removing these causes. One or two additional suggestions are in order, however:

1. *Avoid putting children in situations in which they are tempted to lie*. For example, do not ask them questions that tempt them to give an answer that is pleasing to us. Don't try to pin them down as to the actual facts in a situation. If they want us to know them, they will tell us; in fact they are more likely to do so if we do not seem to be especially concerned about knowing them.

2. *Trust children to tell the truth*. Show them we have confidence in their honesty. We may be "taken in" occasionally, but this is far better than to have them feel that we always are suspicious of them and doubtful of the truth of their comments. When they tell us something, let us accept it without question. To ask too many

questions about it will give them the impression we do not believe them.

3. *If the lying increases in frequency and is so obvious we cannot ignore it, let our children know gently and calmly that they are not fooling us.* Let's not scold them or tell them they are "bad." Let them know that we realize something may be bothering them and that if they will tell us what the trouble is we will do all we can to help them. It should be kept in mind, however, that they may not know why they resort to falsehoods. It will then be our task to return to the questions suggested above and see if we cannot remove the causes that may be responsible for the lying.

4. *Be sure that in the home we are honest and above-board in all of our relationships with our children.* If our children know that we always tell the truth, we may feel fairly certain that they will not develop a permanent habit of telling lies.

CHAPTER 8

Dealing with Problems of Society

In a christian home it may be expected that the members of the family will have a sensitivity to human need wherever it may be found; that they will see the social implications of the gospel of Christ. To that end parents will be concerned about helping their children learn to face realistically and intelligently the problems of racial prejudice and discrimination, economic and political injustice, the use of alcoholic beverages, and narrow nationalism.

It is important that parents should have clearly in mind the qualities of mind and heart children must develop if they are to possess social sensitivity. They are:

1. *A genuine love and respect for all persons, regardless of race, color, or creed.*

2. *A desire to know all the facts about any situation in society that adversely affects persons.*

3. *The habit of evaluating customs, agencies, activities, and laws in the light of their contribution to human welfare.*

4. *Convictions that have their foundation in knowledge and careful evaluation of the facts.*

5. *Open-mindedness—tolerance of the viewpoints of others—a real desire to find out why others think and feel as they do.*

6. *A sense of group responsibility.*

7. *The courage to act in accordance with one's convictions.*

8. *The faith that God helps those who try to better the welfare of mankind.*

It is a pretty big order to guide children so they will develop these qualities. Nevertheless, it must and can be done. Let it be remembered that throughout this book may be found suggestions that are pertinent to this task. For example, it is only as boys and girls have a sense of emotional security that they are genuinely able to forget themselves and to care for and co-operate with others. The ability to get along with others, an appreciation of Jesus and his teachings, and a vital worship experience all prepare the way for the social sensitivity we are now considering.

Parents will keep in mind, also, the ways by which children learn. In the development of social attitudes they are particularly influenced by the example of those in the home, not so much by the words of the parents—although these are important—as by their everyday behavior. The casual remarks of other adults, the caricature of races in funny books, movies, and radio or television programs, and the customs of the community all help determine the attitudes children assume toward social issues.

The most significant social learning takes place, however, in concrete situations in which children have the experience of sharing and co-operating with others, of becoming acquainted with those of other races, of gaining information about how people live, and of facing frankly and honestly the social problems of their community.

Developing Appreciation of Other Races

Perhaps at no other time in the history of our country has it been so imperative for boys and girls to develop an understanding of and appreciation for those of other races. No longer are the minority races of the world willing to submit passively to the scornful superiority or the

104

condescending charity of the white race. They want justice and respect.

The race problem will not be an easy one to solve. We can be certain, however, that it will be solved only as men and women of different races who understand and respect one another work together in the light of Christian principles to overcome racial prejudice and injustice. Therefore, let us begin now to "grow" a generation of boys and girls who have this understanding and respect.

Someone may remark that such a goal is absurd and unrealistic; that racial prejudice and antagonism are natural and never can be eradicated. Nothing could be further from the truth. One is not born with racial prejudice; it is learned.

Some of the ways by which we may help our sons and daughters develop an appreciation of other races are as follows:

1. *By showing appreciation and respect for them ourselves.* This is of supreme importance, as children tend to reflect the viewpoints of their parents.

2. *By having in the home educated and cultured representatives of other races.* Children are likely to think of other races in terms of their least desirable representatives. They need to know that there are Mexicans who are not section hands and Chinese who are not laundrymen, respectable though such work may be.

3. *By studying the customs and habits of other peoples.* *The National Geographic* as well as denominational missionary magazines and the missionary units of the church school will be of invaluable aid. Plan for periods in the home when you sing the songs of other nations and play the games their children play. Encourage your children to collect dolls representing other nationalities.

4. *By encouraging children to find out about the*

achievements of individuals of other races. In addition to becoming acquainted with such world-wide and national figures as Kagawa, George Washington Carver, and Ralph Bunche, suggest that they find out if there are not in your own community peoples of other races whose accomplishments merit attention. Show admiration and appreciation for the artistic accomplishments of other peoples as expressed in paintings, poetry, and music.

5. *By avoiding reference to those of other races by disparaging nicknames such as Chinks, Niggers, Wops, and Greasers.* Avoid jokes which hold up other races to ridicule. Many of the jokes about colored people are of this nature.

6. *By discussing with children the reasons for racial prejudice.*

7. *By taking time to evaluate with them the ideas of other races portrayed over the television or radio, in the movies and in the funnies.*

8. *By helping them in their imagination to picture themselves as members of a minority race and then asking,* "*How would I want to be treated?*" The value of this method is limited, of course, as one cannot really place himself in the position of another with all the emotional accompaniments of membership in a minority group.

9. *By stressing again and again the Christian conviction that God has no favorites, that he loves alike all races of men, and that all men are brothers.*

A Wholesome Concern for Economic Problems

Sometime during the life of a child he is likely to have an experience that will make him keenly aware of the economic inequalities of our day, an experience that may bring forth the spontaneous observation, "It doesn't seem fair." "Why is it," he will ask, "that some people have so much and others so little?" Let us hope that he adds, "What can be done to change the situation?"

Our particular responsibility is to help boys and girls look at such problems as poverty, unemployment, wages, working conditions, child labor, and disputes between management and labor in the light of their effect upon human welfare. We want them to become so concerned about social inequalities and injustice that they will be filled with a burning and lasting zeal to find the Christian solution for them. Here are a few suggestions to keep in mind:

1. *At all times let those in the home show respect for the humblest of workers.*

2. *Help boys and girls realize that many poor and underprivileged people are in no way responsible for their condition.* It is vicious to assume that poverty is always an indication of laziness and shiftlessness, or of dissipation.

3. *Help them realize, also, that many leaders in industry are vitally concerned about the welfare of the workers and are trying to discover ways by which social injustice and inequalities may be eradicated.*

4. *Encourage boys and girls to share with the less privileged, but guard against their developing a feeling of superiority as they do so.* Let there be a sharing of prized possessions rather than merely worn-out toys or old clothes.

5. *Consider with them ways by which they may help the boys and girls in their school who are from poor families feel at home and wanted.*

6. *Discuss with them the causes of poverty, depressions, unemployment, inflation, and labor disputes.* Deal with the social forces that are responsible for them. Avoid blaming individuals and groups.

7. *Consider as objectively as possible various solutions proposed for these problems.* What is our own government doing? Why do some favor its efforts while others oppose them? Try to be fair and impartial in your treatment of these problems and possible solutions. Be neither pro-labor nor pro-management. Try to be pro-Christian.

8. *Help your children get acquainted with conditions in your own city that should be changed, such as unwhole-*

some living conditions, lack of playground facilities for certain groups, and unsanitary situations.

9. *Show the progress that has been made in solving these problems.* For example, note the laws concerning child labor, women in industry, safety devices in factories, the pure food laws, and the right of labor to organize. Boys and girls should not have a hopeless or a helpless feeling with respect to social problems.

10. *Encourage the study of these problems in the church school.*

Facing the Liquor Problem

Our boys and girls more than those of any other generation are subjected constantly to a barrage of attractive and subtle advertising, the purpose of which is to make the use of alcoholic beverages seem desirable. The same influences are lessening the convictions of many adults who once felt keenly the evil of the liquor traffic. Let us not minimize the effect upon boys and girls of this attractive advertising in magazines and papers, of radio announcements of sporting events sponsored by brewing companies, of sparkling glasses of alcoholic beverages consumed by personable individuals on television, of pictures of "men of distinction," and of attractive family scenes in which may always be found glasses of the "drink of moderation."

This is too serious a matter for parents to consider lightly. Unfortunately, because the fight against the liquor traffic has drawn in a few "fanatics," there are people who hesitate to take a stand lest they too be considered queer. But we parents must show our convictions and the reasons for them. In the face of glamorous modern pressures our children will hardly take our stand seriously if it seems to be based on mere prejudice or personal preference. It is our responsibility to acquaint our children with the personal and social consequences of using alcoholic beverages. They will recognize, without our telling "sob" stories or using the "Ten Nights in a Barroom" approach, the misery and degradation that accompany excessive drinking. But they will need the help of facts and figures to realize clearly how people become excessive drinkers—such figures as the percentage of alcoholics who got their start from drinks served in homes, and such facts as the narcotic effects of alcohol that prompted a doctor to tell his son, "If you don't take the first drink, you'll never be a drunkard." We will want to call their attention to such facts as the percentage of automobile accidents for which liquor is a contributing factor, to the relaxing of one's moral inhibitions which liquor frequently brings about, to the general overthrowing of social restraints that liquor tends to encourage, and to crimes for which liquor is largely responsible. You will let them know that it is for such reasons as these that you feel that the use of alcoholic beverages conflicts with one's deepest religious insights and the attempt to live as Christ would have us live.

In our opposition to the use of liquor, however, we need to guard against giving our children the impression that all who drink become drunkards and that all who drink are "bad" men and women. If we give this impression, as children discover that some of the highly respected people in the community and nation drink occasionally and never to excess, they will tend to discount all that we have said about the use of alcoholic beverages. To grant that some respectable people drink need not lessen the effectiveness of our own conviction that the use of alcoholic beverages is harmful; furthermore, it will better prepare our children to face the problem in later years.

It should be remembered, however, that knowledge alone about the consequences of alcohol is not a sufficient motivation for total abstinence. We need to help our boys and girls develop a philosophy of life that leads them to seek the highest values and to work for worthy purposes. Religious insights enable one to see liquor in its proper perspective. One who has dedicated himself to Christ and the cause of his Kingdom knows the answer to this problem.

It will be well to anticipate with our children some of the situations they may face away from home in which they will be tempted to use alcoholic beverages. Boys and girls may take their first drink because they do not know how to get out of doing so without incurring the ridicule and displeasure of their comrades. Let us give specific suggestions, therefore, as to how to refuse a drink without embarrassment either to others or to oneself. This is what the young people wanted who asked a speaker to consider with them the question, "How to say 'No' to liquor on ————campus?" A boy going away to college will be interested in knowing how his dad dealt with the liquor problem when he went to college. One father, for example, shared with his children how, in a fraternity where there were many opportunities and some pressure to drink, he managed through good humor and tact to turn aside the urgings of his friends while keeping their affection and respect.

Building International-Mindedness

These are days in which an internationally-minded citizenry is absolutely essential if peace is to be maintained. Let's not abandon in our own thinking the right of people everywhere to an abundant life. Our boys and girls can readily appreciate the interdependence of nations and understand that as the world grows smaller because of the rapidity of transportation there will be need for even greater co-operation among nations. Neither will it be difficult for them to realize that the kind of co-operation necessary may call for financial sacrifice by some of the more powerful nations. Create in them a willingness to do without in order that those in other parts of the world may have sufficient food and clothing. The use of our surplus wheat for the starving millions in India is a case in point. The giving of a CARE package as a family project, the money coming from savings out of the allowances of all, can be of real value.

Let's send our children out into the world with the habit of keeping informed about public affairs and with the conviction that through their influence upon others and through the ballot, they may help make this world a better place in which to live.

CHAPTER 9

Helping Children Grow Spiritually

W<small>HEN?</small> <small>WHAT?</small> <small>HOW?</small> <small>THESE AND MANY OTHER</small> questions quickly spring to our lips as we think of our responsibility for helping our sons and daughters learn about God and Jesus. How old should they be before they hear of God? What shall we teach about his nature and how he works in the world? What shall our attitude be toward their innumerable questions? How shall we present Jesus to them? These are not merely academic questions. They get right down to where you and I live.

First of all, let us look at this matter of *when*. There are those who state quite frankly that the idea of God is so beyond the possibility of a small child to comprehend that all reference to him should be omitted until the age of seven or eight. Others, however, granting that a little child will not be able to have a very adequate concept of God, nevertheless feel that it would not only be impossible but undesirable to keep children away from any contact with him until the age of seven. They insist, and some of us feel rightly so, that a child can develop a feeling of love for and dependence upon God long before he fully understands him. After all, the endeavor to comprehend God is a lifelong quest that is never completed.

In helping children learn about God and Jesus we should keep in mind the following:

1. *During the early years children should have experiences that will prepare the way for an understanding of God.* These experiences will arise largely out of their as-

sociation with members of the family. They will experience the *love* of parents, and in turn they will have feelings of love for them. They must be helped to identify these experiences and their own feelings with the term love, if that term is to have any meaning for them as it is used later to describe God's character. They will learn to rejoice in the *dependability* of their parents, in their *wisdom* and in their *power*. They will observe their *fairness* and their willingness to *sacrifice* for others. As these terms, too, are identified with the experiences, boys and girls increasingly become able to understand what is meant by a God of love, dependability, wisdom, and fairness. Little children first think of God in terms of the characteristics they see manifested in their fathers and mothers.

2. *Children's first experiences with God should be in connection with happy events and in terms of what he does and wants.* As parents and children joyfully explore the wonders of nature, how natural it is to thank God the creator for making such a wonderful and interesting world. It was a wise mother who began to sing softly, "Thank you, God, for the moon," as her children gazed in delight and awe at the brilliant full moon.

As the family has other happy experiences together, boys and girls may be led to realize that God wants everyone to be as happy as they are. As they take care of pets, prepare the soil for the seeds, and co-operate in the home, children are learning that God wants them to co-operate with and be helpful to others. They begin to realize that God works through his laws and that the sunlight, the rich earth, the refreshing rain, and the work of the gardener all are the means by which he makes a beautiful flower to grow.

3. *Avoid associating unhappy experiences with God.*

Children who are told that God is watching them every minute to see if they are good—that he has his big eye upon them—frequently develop a horror and fear of God that remains throughout life. The prayer, "Now I lay me down to sleep," for many a sensitive child has linked the thought of God indelibly with the thought of death. It was a terrified youngster who, while looking into the fire with his aunt, shuddered and said, "Auntie, if you aren't good, God will burn you up." Such ideas of God make it difficult for children to love and have confidence in him.

4. *Be prepared to answer their questions about God.* They are certain to come—such questions as, What is God? Where is God? What keeps God up in the sky? How can God be everywhere at once? and, What is God doing now? Obviously all of them cannot be answered satisfactorily. The correct answer to some would have no meaning for them as they have not yet had the experiences necessary for such an understanding. Other questions are unanswerable, as after all there are mysteries of life that man cannot fathom. It is not easy, for example, to explain to an inquiring child how God hears us. Many of the questions are asked on the spur of the moment and do not represent a real concern. Others are purely speculative. It is our responsibility, however, to make every effort to answer them in such a way that there will be a minimum of confusion and uncertainty in their thinking.

Answering Questions

We prepare ourselves to answer these questions by clarifying our own thinking with reference to our own beliefs. First of all we need to be sure of the things that we most surely know and believe about God. For example, we believe that he loves all races, that he is fair, and that he works through the laws of nature and through social relationships. We also need to be certain of that which we do not believe. Some of us do not believe, let us say, that God sends war to punish mankind, or that he "strikes down dead" those who disobey him. A child who comes from public school with such a query, as one did, we are able to answer immediately. Finally, we should be aware of ideas and speculations about which we are still uncertain, but about which, also, we are still trying to find out. How God hears prayer, for example, may be a question that we are unable to answer dogmatically.

In answering questions we will remember that children will believe us literally. Therefore we will always be honest, never telling them something we ourselves do not believe. When we do not know the answers, we will be quite frank so to indicate. In addition, however, we will help boys and girls realize that the finding out about God and how he works in the world is a family quest and that each member of the family can share with the others his growing insights. In answering questions, also, we will answer the specific question only, will avoid generalizing, and will keep from raising new questions. If we do this, children will return to us for help when additional questions occur to them.

What Is God?

Perhaps the most difficult questions to answer are these: Who is God? Where is God? and, What is God like? If children have had some of the stories of Jesus given to them and if they know something about his love for children, his interest in others, and his courage, it may be said that God is like Jesus. Care needs to be taken, however, lest the child become confused in his thinking about God and Jesus. He should be helped to see that Jesus teaches us about God and tells us what God is like. Jesus speaks of God primarily as a Father.

Jesus taught that God is a Spirit. Shall we attempt to help children think of him in this way? Many would not do so as they think the term "spirit" suggests ghosts and fairies. Others feel that this need not necessarily be the case. Granting that the term is a difficult one for children to comprehend, it is felt that the term may gradually have meaning poured into it for children. They may be helped to see that it is not the body of the mother or father that loves them, for example; flesh and blood are simply chemical substances. It is that intangible something in them that loves and appreciates and sacrifices, and it is this that we call the spirit. These spirits of ours express themselves through our bodies or by means of them, but are more than our bodies. When the child wants to do a helpful deed, it is his spirit that prompts him to do it.

All of this is pretty strong meat for children and certainly should not be presented to them until they are asking sincere questions about the nature of God. Those who have used this approach, however, have discovered that it has proved to be helpful to children. A nine-year-old boy helped answer the questions of his six-year-old brother concerning a spirit by telling him that our spirits live in our bodies in the same way that we live in a house. When the house is worn out, we move away; when our body wears out, the spirit leaves it. This same boy had been comforted several years before when his puppy died by the thought that the spirit is something separate from the body. Although the term was still somewhat puzzling to him, as was to be expected, he was growing in his understanding of it and hence in his understanding of God.

Another suggestion is that we shall help children think

of God as being like some of the intangibles of life. A child knows there is the time of the year that we call spring, but he can't put his hand on it or feel it. He can, however, see what spring does and the differences it makes in the buds, flowers, and birds. Love is another of the intangibles. We can't touch it, but we can feel it in what it does for us. So it is with God. We can't actually see him, but we can see his handiwork in nature and his Spirit expressing itself in the lives of devoted men, women, and children.

However we may describe the nature and reality of God to children, they are likely to be somewhat perplexed. Let us not be too disturbed if questions continue to plague them. Neither let us become perturbed if they think of God in terms of a physical person. There is a great difference in deliberately teaching a child that God has a physical body and in overlooking his anthropomorphic idea of God. It is not always necessary to correct every inadequate idea of God a child may have. At times we should, of course, and we will take advantage of every opportunity to add meaning to the idea of God as a spiritual power or as one of the intangibles of life.

5. *Do not be disturbed by adolescent doubts.* Adolescents are beginning to think for themselves. They may find that they no longer can accept some of the childish ideas of God they once had—especially their anthropomorphic concept of him. In getting rid of these they may begin to doubt the existence of God altogether. Be patient with them. Share your own reasons for believing in God and your own experiences of fellowship with him. Do not make them feel sinful because of their doubts. After all, it frequently is through doubts that one reaches his own faith. Encourage them to do their own thinking and to find a faith of their own, even though their own con-

clusions may not agree in their entirety with yours. They will appreciate and respond to your patience and understanding.

6. *Boys and girls should grow in their appreciation of and devotion to Jesus.* Although it seems almost sacrilegious to say so, it should be kept in mind that boys and girls get tired of having Jesus always held up as an example —as one who never did anything wrong. If the miraculous aspects of his life are stressed over and over again, they tend to think of him primarily as a wonder-worker, rather than as a real, live, flesh and blood boy and man who had experiences similar to their own. Jesus as a wonder-worker appears to them as a vague, unreal sort of person.

Let us present Jesus, therefore, as an attractive, fun-loving, wide-awake boy who really grew in stature, in mind, and in favor with God and man. Let them think of him as a vigorous, energetic, and understanding person. They feel no special pull toward a Jesus who is "gentle and mild." His understanding and love of children, however, his delightful sense of humor, his masterful leadership of his disciples, and his physical and moral courage do appeal to them. They will be interested in and see the significance of many of the stories he told. If they also find that their parents find in Jesus a living reality and are seeking to attain his spirit, they, too, are likely to find in him one whom they will want to follow.

Learning to Pray

Christian homes will provide the kind of atmosphere and the personal guidance that will enable boys and girls to find in worship not only an intensely satisfying and enriching experience, but a growing one as well. Prayer is at the heart of the worship experience, and we will be concerned, therefore, about helping our children develop a vital prayer life. In teaching them to pray let us keep in mind the following:

1. *Begin early*. There are those who feel that the child should see and hear his parents pray—the father as well as the mother—long before he understands what they are doing. As he is tucked into bed at night during the first two or three years, let the parents pause for a moment to thank God for such a fine child and to ask that they may be wise in their guidance of him. As this and other prayers are offered night after night, it is felt that the child will become increasingly aware of what is being done and that a foundation, therefore, is being laid for his own prayers when he becomes older.

2. *Talk over with children the possible content of their prayers.* The "good-night talk," which can become a very happy experience for both parents and children, furnishes an excellent opportunity to do this. Some of the events of the day for which one is thankful may be recalled. Difficulties that have arisen among members of the family may be mentioned and suggestions given by both parents and children as to how they may be avoided on the morrow. It may be decided, for example, to ask God to help Jimmy to remember to let Mary play with his sled, and to help Mary remember to put it away in the basement when she is through with it. All this can be done without creating in children a harmful sense of guilt or leading them to become unduly introspective.

3. *Spontaneous and informal prayers are more desirable than memorized or formal ones.* Remember how quickly when you were a child you could say, "Now I lay me down to sleep?" Some of us could rush through it in a hurry! And yet we thought we had prayed, when in reality we had only "said our prayers." Let's keep our boys and girls

from getting into such a stereotyped and artificial pattern of prayer. Talking with them about what to include in their prayers leads them quite naturally to express their thoughts in their own words. Let's encourage them to do so.

As children grow older, we may occasionally want to read to them beautiful and appropriate prayers. They should gain some knowledge of the gems of devotional literature. But here again let us guard against the tendency of a child to memorize such prayers and substitute them for his own. A boy of five was growing in his ability to express grace in his own words at the table. Then he learned a special prayer of thanks at the kindergarten. From that time until he was twelve the memorized grace was the only one he used. Thus it definitely interfered with growth in his ability to use the language of prayer.

A few observations about the form and language of prayer may be appropriate. Encourage children to address their prayers to God. Surely this is what Jesus would have them do. Remember that the child's span of attention is short, so the prayer should be short. The use of the words *you* and *your* with reference to God makes a prayer more natural than does the use of the terms *thee* and *thy*. Use specific rather than general terms. For example, to thank God for a pretty rose is more meaningful to a child than to thank him for flowers; to ask God to help him remember to let Harry play with his blocks is far more significant than to ask that he remember to be unselfish.

The posture children should assume in prayer may be left to the personal preference of children and parents. Some will want to kneel at the bedside, others will pray as they are lying in bed, and still others may pray while in a sitting posture with their heads bowed.

4. *Prayer should be in harmony with one's idea of God*

121

and of how he works in the world. Expressions of gladness, a "Thank you, God," for something the child likes, or just talking to God about anything that interests him, fits in with our idea of God as a personal friend and as the

Creator of the universe. These are the prayers we may expect small children to pray and that we should encourage.

Any false ideas of God and of how he works in the world will usually find expression in children's prayers. A child prays that the rain will stop so he can play outdoors, or he asks God for a tricycle. In other words, he thinks of God as more or less a celestial Santa Claus. Our clue, then, is to watch for an opportunity to talk with him about how God works in the world, and how he makes his good gifts available to us. For example, if he prays for rain to stop so he can play, we will tell him in simple terms how God has created rain and other natural processes of weather and soil to provide us with food and drink; we will also tell him in terms that he can understand about some of the laws that govern weather. As he comes to understand these things, we may lead him to thank God for the rain and to ask for help in playing happily indoors. If he prays for a tricycle, we will help him see that God has provided parents to take care of children, to give them food, shelter, clothing, and even such things as tricycles when they can be afforded. Then he may be guided to pray about his own responsibilities in the family economy.

It is important that children realize that God may expect them to help him answer their prayers. Certainly they should not be led to rely on God to save them from their own carelessness and irresponsibility. It is unfortunate, for example, when they are taught to ask God to keep them from harm while crossing a street. It is far better for them to ask God to help them to remember to be careful in crossing the street. It was a wise mother who when her son prayed that God would keep his puppy from being run over by a car led him through conversation to the place where he prayed instead that God would help him remember to keep the front gate closed so that the puppy couldn't get out into the street and be run over.

5. *Prayer should not be limited to a special time or place*. Invaluable as is the habit of regular evening prayer, children should not get the idea that prayer is to be limited to that time or place. Parents will be on the alert, therefore, for experiences during the day in which prayer will

be natural and meaningful. Any interesting, new experience—especially with nature—affords such an opportunity. Stress may be placed upon the value of developing the habit of praying frequently throughout the day. Such prayers will be brief—consisting perhaps of only one sentence—but they will be significant. It means much if one is in the habit of asking for self-control when about to become angry, or for courage when tempted. God becomes a companion if one is in the habit of thinking of him in connection with happy experiences, and of talking with him, however briefly, about one's problems.

6. *Let there be growth in the prayer life.* As boys and girls grow mentally and spiritually, their childish prayers will be superseded by prayers that reflect that growth. To be sure, prayers of thankfulness and fellowship will continue throughout life. But increasingly the needs of others —and of the world—will be lifted up in prayer with the petition that God may help them discover what they can do to meet these needs. Prayers will become decreasingly self-centered, thus reflecting a growing social sensitivity.

Aids to Worship

Let us remember that a person does not decide "all at once" to worship. We can scarcely say to our boys and girls without any preparation whatsoever, "Go to, now, pray!" An attitude of reverence toward God, of thankfulness, and a desire to pray arise out of experiences that are meaningful. It is important, therefore, that we provide in our homes the kinds of stimuli that tend to produce the desire to worship.

Objects of nature, as well as books in this field, frequently are helpful in developing a worshipful attitude. A growing plant, beautiful flowers, a singing canary, and even collections of bugs or snakes are of value. One family reports that one of their most worshipful experiences occurred as they gathered about a cicada that was bursting out of its shell. As it gradually pushed its way out and unfolded its delicate wings, they talked about the wonderful world God has made and had a brief prayer of thankfulness in which the children wholeheartedly joined.

A mother reports that a book on rocks and minerals written for fourth-grade children proved to be one of the most inspiring that ever came into their home. After she had read from this book to her small son at the devotional hour, the boy closed his evening prayer with these words, "Thank you, God, for making iron. I think it's the best thing you ever did."

The Bible

Christian parents will make a special effort to find out how the Bible may be made meaningful to boys and girls. After their children are four years old, they may want to purchase some of the more desirable Bible storybooks, remembering that some of the most readily available are the least desirable. They will guard against introducing children too early to stories which have spiritual meanings that are beyond their comprehension. To do so tends to make them indifferent to these stories later on because they are "old stuff."

As children reach the age of nine or ten, they should be helped to see the Bible stories in their original setting and to think of the Bible as the record of God's continuing revelation to man and man's struggle to find God. At that age they are interested in finding out how the Bible came to be and in seeing how modern versions differ from the authorized. They should be helped to find in the experiences of the men and women in the Bible suggestions that will help them in their own thinking and everyday relationships. Now is the time to give them a Bible of their own and a good book about the Bible. For younger children, Bowie's *The Bible Story for Boys and Girls*, and for older boys and girls and youth, his book, *The Story of the Bible*, are invaluable.

Parents should use their own ingenuity and imagination in discovering ways in which the Bible may be used in a natural and interesting way in the home. Here are but a few of the many possibilities:

1. *Follow the suggestions to parents found in most church-school materials.* Small children will enjoy having read to them again the stories read at church school. Older children will appreciate help in church-school projects or activities that include a study of or use of the Bible.

2. *Informal Bible quizzes or games may be used to find out how much is known by members of the family about the Bible.* Interest is enhanced if boys and girls are encouraged to ask questions, as well as to try to answer them. Such quizzes, for example, may ask questions about the location of books of the Bible, the authors of well-known quotations or stories, the life and teachings of specific Bible characters, or the different versions of the Bible. One should guard against quizzes that deal primarily with unrelated facts and thus have little meaning for children.

3. *Plan for a definite time for Bible study, once a day or once or twice a week.* Suggestions for such a study are: (*a*) one of the smaller books of the Bible such as Ruth, Philemon, or one of the Gospels; (*b*) the life and teaching of an interesting person in the Bible; (*c*) Bible times and customs and their reflection in the stories found in the Bible; (*d*) how the Bible came to be written; (*e*) ideas found in the Bible about topics selected by members of the family, such as God, prayer, attitudes toward others, right and wrong; (*f*) how different versions came into being

and how they differ from each other. Guard against letting such a study become burdensome or boresome. When assignments are made, let older members be asked to work with younger members.

4. *Dramatize some of the gospel stories or some of the more desirable of the Old Testament stories.*

5. *Make a collection of great religious paintings.* Using a book such as *The Gospel in Art,* by Albert Edward Bailey, have a discussion on how well each member of the family thinks the artist represented the Bible story.

6. *Capitalize upon your children's experience with choral reading in the public schools and see how well members of the family can read together one of the psalms.*

7. *Study favorite songs and hymns to discover the references to Bible verses or incidents contained in them.*

8. *Encourage your children to listen to "The Greatest Story Ever Told," or the "Radio Edition of the Bible."*

9. *Let there be occasions on which each member of the family may place on the worship center a Bible opened to his favorite verse or story.*

A Worship Center

Many families are discovering that a worship center in the home is a definite aid to worship. The making of such a center may well be a family project participated in by old and young. The center may be on a table on which is an open Bible, a wooden cross, or a beautiful picture flanked by two candles that are lighted for the worship period. Some families have a candle for each member of the family; and as that member comes down in the morning, he pauses for a moment at the worship center in prayer and then lights his candle. Each member of the family, therefore, as he looks at the lighted candles of the others, feels that tie that binds their hearts in Christian love. There may be devotional books, books of Bible stories, or even the church-school lesson material on the worship table. In some cases young people like to have special worship centers in their own rooms.

It may be assumed that in the Christian home there will be periods when the family worships together. It is not so much the method or the frequency of these worship experiences that is important as it is the significance of the experience for those participating in them. Some families will have family worship every day, others twice a week, and still others only once a week. In planning for these periods we should keep in mind the following:

1. *Over a period of time every member of the family should have a share in planning for them.*

2. *Let the experience be linked with the everyday activities and problems of the family.* Look at these in the light of Christian principles. Prayers may then be related to these experiences and to the problems of each member of the group.

3. *Let there be variety in the kind of services held.* From time to time the services should include the reading of the Bible, the telling of Bible stories, the presenting of interesting information about God's world, the singing of hymns, the study of pictures, the discussion of problems, and the reading of poems.

4. *As a rule it is desirable to build the worship service about a central theme.*

5. *Use printed helps intelligently.* The special worship materials in magazines for the family or carefully selected booklets such as *Thoughts of God for Boys and Girls* will be especially helpful. Many constructive suggestions for these services may be found in *The Family Worships Together,* by Mazelle Wildes Thomas. Materials should always be adapted to the particular needs of your family.

CHAPTER 10

Developing an Appreciation of the Church

$\mathcal{T}$HERE ARE PARENTS WHO SEND THEIR CHILDREN TO church school and then wash their hands of any further responsibility for guiding their religious development. As we have come to a more adequate understanding of all that is involved in the guidance of religious growth, perhaps we, too, at times have wished that we could complacently turn over this responsibility to the church. We realize, of course, that this cannot be done. The home is the most vital agency for Christian teaching, and parents are the most effective teachers. We would not have it otherwise, although it places a tremendous responsibility upon us.

The Church Helps Parents

Conceding the supreme importance of the home does not mean that we need to minimize the value of the church. Let us thank God that it stands ever-ready to help us guide the growing religious life of our children.

Glance for a moment at what the church will do. It will help our children learn how to worship and to develop adequate ideas of God. Its leaders will guide them into constructive activities that promote a sense of group responsibility, that develop increasing sensitivity to human need, and that motivate them to be more co-operative in the home. The church will help boys and girls to form noble purposes and to discover criteria for determining right from wrong. It will surround them with wholesome influences from childhood through old age.

The church will do all this, that is, if boys and girls have a real appreciation for it. If they don't like it, if they find its services uninteresting, or if they become indifferent to it, its influence upon them will be negligible. How important it is, therefore, that we help them develop a love and appreciation for the church.

Perhaps our first responsibility is to help create among the leaders of our own local church a willingness to put money and effort into the kind of educational program that will appeal to boys and girls. Altogether too many adults consider the work of the church school to be of secondary importance. Many of them want their children to receive the same kind of teaching they received in their childhood. They forget that there has been progress in educational method and in an understanding of the Bible and of the implications of the Christian gospel. They would not for one moment think of sending their children to a secular school that was conducted as were schools of fifty years ago. We need to help them see this and to throw their support behind a well-planned program of Christian education.

To this end let us become acquainted with the facilities of our church school. Are the classrooms pleasant and large enough to care comfortably for those in attendance? Do the teachers have the proper literature, blackboards, visual resources, and other equipment to make their teaching effective? Are they encouraged to take special training each year for their work?

Let us remember that children are comparing the church school with the public school and that in many cases such comparisons are unfavorable to the church school. A seven-year-old boy frankly said to his father, "Daddy, I don't like church school as well as I do my other school." When asked why this was the case, he replied, "Because we don't do as many interesting things at church school." Children sometimes feel that the church school isn't very important because nothing significant is accomplished there.

Parents Co-operate with Teachers

It is important that we know the purposes and plans of the teachers of our children and discover ways by which we may co-operate with them and undergird their teachings in the life of the home. Our church-school leaders are recommending meetings between teachers and parents for this very purpose. At such meetings, which may be held quarterly, consideration should be given to the unit of work for the coming quarter and suggestions given as to how parents may co-operate in it. Parents will have an opportunity to ask the teachers questions about the use of the Bible, the value of projects, and particular behavior problems that may have come to their notice. Out of the study and fellowship of such meetings there develops a spirit of sympathy, understanding, and harmony between parents and teachers.

One illustration of such co-operation may be of value. A class of junior children under the guidance of a skilled teacher decided to become better acquainted with the activities of their denomination in their city. They visited several of the denominational settlements in the community. Attention was called to the home and the surroundings of those whom the settlements served. Maps were secured that showed the areas of the city where disease, poverty, and crime were most prevalent. Other maps revealed that in these areas there were few recreational facilities or parks. The children came to the conclusion, therefore, that there is some relationship between disease, crime, and poverty and the lack of recreational facilities.

In addition to getting the facts the children were helped to realize that those living in underprivileged areas were not necessarily inferior to others, but that it was difficult for them to rise above their surroundings. They saw how the church was attempting to serve these groups. As a result of the study they came to an appreciation of the responsibility of the church for the underprivileged and were given opportunities to do something for them.

This study could not have been the success that it was without the co-operation of the parents. It involved the use of cars and the attendance of children upon weekday sessions of the class. It was successful because the parents were willing for their children to take part in a worthwhile experiment.

A mother reports that each week she reviews with her children the church-school material used on the preceding Sunday. This not only acquaints her with the literature but helps her children realize that she is interested in the work of the church school and considers it to be significant. Many of the stories and lessons may be saved for use at a later date. Some families use the stories and the biblical material in the church-school literature for the family devotional periods during the week.

Educational leaders are saying to church-school teachers, "Get into the homes of your children. Know their parents. Get acquainted with the interests and hobbies of your boys and girls. Go on hikes with them. Do not limit your activities with them to the Sunday morning session." Knowing this, let us not wait for teachers always to take the initiative. Let us invite them into our homes and encourage their outside classroom contacts with our children.

It is exceedingly desirable that boys and girls shall learn to think of their minister as a personal friend. Too frequently parents think of the pastor's visit primarily in terms of their own interests or needs. Let us give him an opportunity to talk with our children, to see their collections, and even to play with them. One pastor won the heart of a young boy by telling him of his experiences

with snakes. To that boy the pastor was no longer simply the man who stood in the pulpit on Sunday and preached. He was a personal friend, interested in the same things that interested him. Because of this the boy listened with more attention and appreciation to his friend in the pulpit.

When Should Children Attend?

There is considerable difference of opinion as to the age at which a child should be taken to the morning worship service. On the one hand there are those who would have parents take two- or three-year-olds to church. They realize that these children will not be able to understand much that is going on, but they feel they will catch something of value from the atmosphere of the church service and, most important, will develop the habit of going to church.

On the other hand there are those who remind us that the average church service is primarily for adults. The hymns, prayers, scripture readings, and sermon are slanted toward adults rather than toward children. Furthermore, it is not only exceedingly difficult but most undesirable for most children to remain quiet for an hour at a time. Their span of attention is short and their demand for physical activity great. How much better it is, this group feels, for small children to remain in the nursery and for older children to remain in the expanded session of the church school where they have opportunities for study, play, fellowship, and worship that meet their own particular needs. If children have happy experiences at church during these early years, they will look forward to the time when they will begin to worship with the congregation.

Here are some general principles that govern church attendance for children that may be helpful:

1. *If our church makes provision for children during the morning worship service by means of a nursery and an expanded session, we should by all means avail ourselves of this opportunity.*

2. *If our small children want to go to the service and seem to find satisfaction in it, there is no reason why they should not do so.* Children differ considerably in their nervous systems and in their likes and dislikes. Whereas most children get restless and nervous if made to keep quiet for an hour, some do not.

3. *If we find that the child we are taking to the service is beginning to develop a violent dislike for the church, we should give serious consideration as to what we should do.* There are several possibilities:

a) We can continue to insist that he go to the service each Sunday. If his opposition is mild, no particular harm may be done. On the other hand there is real danger, and this should not be minimized, that he may develop an antagonism toward the church that may remain throughout life. It is not easy to overcome first impressions. Habits that one does not enjoy, furthermore, are easily broken.

b) We can let him stop going altogether. If he is getting satisfaction out of the church-school hour and if we ourselves are active in the life of the church, he probably will want to go as he gets older.

c) We may compromise to the extent of not insisting that he go every Sunday. When he reaches the age of ten or eleven, he may be expected to attend regularly.

Whatever we decide to do about this matter of church attendance for our children, we should keep in mind the fact that our primary purpose should be so to guide them that they will develop a lifelong interest in the church, its activities and its services.

For many families church attendance is a family experience that is accepted without question. It should be remembered even then, however, that children will find the morning worship service of the church significant only to the extent that they are acquainted with the elements that compose it. The pastor is wise if he frequently uses biblical passages and hymns that children have studied in the church school. Parents may suggest to him that he announce or put into the bulletin each Sunday the hymns, scripture passages, responsive readings, and the sermon topic for the following Sunday. During the week, then, families may use these in their family worship services. With such preparation children will be ready to participate in the worship service and find value in it.

Some families may find it interesting to let each member of the family suggest what he thinks the pastor will say in the sermon that is to be based on the selected scripture passages. When the family returns from church, note which member most correctly anticipated the message of the morning. In addition let each member recall that part of the sermon that interested him most. Even sermons for adults may have illustrations that appeal to children.

Boys and girls need to realize that the service is primarily a service of worship and that the sermon is but one part of the service. An eight-year-old boy told his father he did not care to go to church as he did not understand the sermon. The father suggested that some of the greatest values in the service were to be found in the singing, in the listening to the glorious music by the choir, in the study of the beautiful stained-glass windows, and in the chance to be quiet and to think about God. The boy immediately indicated a new interest in the service and expressed a desire to attend it.

Joining the Church

Most boys and girls indicate a desire to join the church somewhere between the ages of nine and twelve. Parents should recognize this decision for what it is—one of the most significant they have made. We will co-operate with the pastor in the class he has for those entering the church. We will show our pride and joy because of their decision. We will talk with them in the home about what it means to be a member of the church. As they take its vows at the altar, we will renew our own vows with them.

Altogether too frequently boys and girls who have joined the church with high expectations lose interest in it because they are given no responsibility for its ongoing program. Therefore let us make every effort to discover ways by which they may come to feel an essential part of it. They may help in the church office, help beautify the lawn, serve on church committees, and act as ushers occasionally at the church services. Intermediates and seniors may have representation on the church board of education or the religious education committee.

Church Family Activities

Churches increasingly are recognizing their responsibility not only to individual members of a family but to the family as a unit. They are providing activities, therefore, in which families as families may participate, such as family nights at church, the Sunday evening family fellowship, church nights at home, church picnics or hikes, and family camps. There are service projects in the area of missions or social welfare, furthermore, which families may accept as a family. Important as it is to have a graded church school and activities that are of special significance for the different age groups in the church, activities participated in by the entire family together are equally important if the church is to be appreciated as it should be by the members of the family. Recognizing this, we will encourage all such attempts to make our church more nearly a "family-centered church."

It should be remembered, also, that we as parents have special needs that the church can meet. It will mean much to us, for example, to have an opportunity for study and fellowship with other parents who are facing problems similar to ours, problems, for example, that are considered in this book. Study classes for parents, family life and marriage clinics, and the use of audio-visual resources that contribute to the understanding of child development and wholesome family living should receive our enthusiastic support.

Finally, let us remember that our sons and daughters will learn to love and to serve the church only as we love and serve it. Let us fail neither them nor the church.

CHAPTER 11

Helping Adolescent Boys and Girls

THROUGHOUT THIS BOOK REFERENCE HAS BEEN MADE from time to time concerning the characteristics and needs of adolescents, and suggestions have been made especially as to ways by which they may be helped to gain emotional maturity. In this chapter we shall be dealing a bit more specifically with some of the problems that adolescents and their parents face.

Parents Become Problems

It is well to note that at about the time children reach the period of adolescence many parents become real problems not only to themselves but to their children as well. They suddenly realize that in a short time their children will leave home for good. They think of all the mistakes they have made as they have tried to guide them through the years. They become frantic and try to rectify these mistakes all at once, sometimes by becoming unusually strict and at other times by becoming exceedingly lenient. As they envision the home with the children gone, they become sorry for themselves. They would snatch the last few moments of happiness with their children. They refuse to let their boys and girls become independent, therefore, and tie them to their apron strings with knots that are firm. If the children refuse to confide in them, they pout; if they reject their advice so freely given, they become martyrs and make no attempt to hide their martyrdom under a bushel! The last years the children have in the home, therefore, often become miserable rather than glorious.

Need Patience and Understanding

Perhaps never before have parents needed to pray so earnestly for wisdom, patience, and courage as when they try to help their boys and girls prepare for the adulthood that is just around the corner. Much of their work has already been done, to be sure, but the later adolescent still desperately needs affection, understanding, and respect. Because of his desire for independence he is likely to become dogmatic in statement, critical of loved ones, and impatient with restraints. If he is having difficulty in his schoolwork and is not being accepted as he would like by his peers, or has failed in achieving some desired goal, he may feel insecure and hostile toward the world in general, a hostility that may reflect itself in disrespectful behavior toward the parents. A girl who isn't having the dates she thinks she ought to have or a boy who just missed making the athletic team may be rather hard to live with for a time. Wise parents at such times will try to avoid situations that will call forth disrespectful behavior and will guard against getting into arguments with them. It will not always be easy to be this patient and understanding. We will feel like "telling them off!" And yet if parents fail their children at this time, they fail them at the most crucial period of life.

Let parents rejoice, therefore, in the growing independence of their sons and daughters. They will not be hurt if their children tend to confide in others more than in them; they will give them the privacy they crave and will not pry into their secrets; they will not be shocked, at least outwardly, by comments obviously made for the purpose of shocking; they will not be critical of their friends, and when their friends are in the home, they, the parents, will stay in the background but will be available if needed.

Now is the time, too, when parents may begin to share with their adolescent boys and girls their own problems, aspirations, and accomplishments. They will take their ideas seriously and will guard against treating them with scornful amusement or studied indifference. If parents show their boys and girls that they respect them as persons, they will feel free to come to them for help.

What About College?

For many boys and girls the matter of going to college will not be a problem; they will go as a matter of course. Not to do so would be considered a disgrace to the family.

Granting that for most boys and girls a college education is desirable, it should be recognized quite frankly that not everyone should go. The young college student referred to earlier, who was preparing for law when he wanted to go into the hotel business, is a case in point. He was making a miserable record, was slow mentally, and obviously was unhappy. Although a college education is of value for most people, regardless of their vocation, this young man was wasting several years of life because his family was more concerned about their pride than about his welfare. Parents should guard against making such a mistake with their children.

By and large, however, boys and girls should be helped to see the desirability of attending college and should be guided in the selection of a college to attend. Here are some questions that should be answered before a final decision is made:

1. *Is the college an institution of recognized standing, approved by the accrediting agencies?*

2. *Is it large enough to have adequate facilities but small*

enough for individual guidance and help from faculty and administrative officials?

3. *Does it have an able faculty in the fields in which the student is particularly interested?*

4. *Is there a wholesome social life on the campus?* Is it necessary to be a member of a fraternity or sorority in order to "rate"?

5. *Is the expense reasonable?* Are there opportunities for remunerative work for those who need to earn part of their expenses?

6. *Do faculty and administrators have a vital concern for the religious welfare and growth of the students?*

7. *Does the curriculum provide opportunities for facing contemporary problems?*

8. *Have the alumni "made good"?*

Sometimes it is a family tradition for its members to attend a particular college or university. There are many who doubt the wisdom of this, as they believe that in such a situation a student tends constantly to feel under pressure to make as good a record as have other members of the family. Furthermore, he is likely always to be known as his father's son, or his brother's brother, and is never accepted as an individual in his own right. All this places a student under an unnecessary emotional strain.

Deciding on a Vocation

A frequent cause of emotional insecurity in adolescents is the fear that they may be unable to make a living. There is real therapeutic value, therefore, in their having a work experience in which by the sweat of their brow they earn money. In some cases it may be desirable for boys and girls to work for a year before going to college. They are likely to appreciate it more when they get there. However, one must guard against permitting boys and girls to drift into their lifework as is so frequently the case with those who "just take a job in order to make some money."

In helping adolescents select their vocation we should keep the following in mind. First of all, one's vocation should be one that he thoroughly enjoys and in which he can be successful. Therefore it is important that adolescents discover what they like to do and can do well. In the second place, a vocation should be socially useful, should contribute to the welfare of mankind. And in the third place, it should offer a real future. Questions such as the following should be asked: Is the vocation overcrowded? Will it provide opportunities for advancement? Will it afford a substantial living? Will it allow time for recreation, cultural pursuits, and participation in social and civic activities? Does it call for creative activity?

Boys and girls should be encouraged to read pamphlets and books that describe various occupations, to talk with people representing various walks of life, to take the vocational aptitude tests given in many of our high schools and colleges, and especially to try out some of the occupations in which they are interested.

Parents, as well as young people, need to realize that one should not rush into his vocation and that some experimentation may be necessary before a final decision may be made. It is not a disgrace to change one's mind about his vocation. Here, for example, is a boy who after two years in an engineering school decided to quit that field and enter into the field of psychology. When such changes are not a means of running away from something that is hard or disagreeable, they are likely to be desirable.

A word to fathers who are eager for their sons to follow in their footsteps: Be careful! Don't insist that they do so or make them feel guilty if they decide otherwise. Many a man has gone through life dissatisfied and unsuccessful because he was afraid to disappoint his father by his vocational choice. If you love your sons, help them find the type of work *they* like.

Selecting a Life Partner

It is to be expected that parents will be tremendously concerned about their children's choice of life partners. Furthermore, it is quite to be expected that they should feel that no boy is worthy of their daughter and that no girl is good enough for their son. But let them keep this conviction to themselves! They must recognize—and this is indeed a *must*—that the choice is not theirs to make; it belongs to the son or the daughter alone. After the choice has been made, parents should be good sports and adjust themselves to it if they are to be fair to their children.

This does not mean, however, that parents have nothing to say about whom their children will marry. Indeed they do. They begin influencing the decision long before the time for the actual decision arrives. The final choice will have its rootage in the high ideals that were cultivated in the home, in the wholesome family life, and in the Christian character that has been developed.

Let us keep close to our boys and girls as they begin to show an interest in the opposite sex. We will provide them with opportunities to meet desirable boys and girls. We will welcome them into our homes. It should be remembered, also, that the first love affairs are not to be taken lightly or to be ridiculed as being merely puppy love. Temporary and fleeting though these experiences may be, they prepare our children for more genuine and lasting love later on.

Boys and girls need and will welcome, if given in the right way, help in deciding how one may be sure he is in love. Let us put into their hands some of the excellent books and pamphlets in this field, such as Burkhart's *From Friendship to Marriage,* Eddy's *Sex and Youth,* and Dahlberg's *Youth and the Homes of Tomorrow.* They will be interested in knowing how we were sure of our life partner. We will remind them that important as is physical attraction, it alone is insufficient to insure a happy marriage. We will help them see that happiness in marriage depends upon such factors as personal congeniality, common interests, a similar philosophy of life and religion, and emotional maturity.

If a boy or a girl is about to make a choice that we are convinced is unwise, we need to remember that to oppose or to criticize is likely to make the choice more certain. In some cases it may be possible, however, to arrange for separations or delays, in the meantime providing new acquaintances that may be attractive. If our boys and girls seek our judgment, we will help them weigh the possibilities for happiness with the contemplated partner, assuring them that the final decision must be theirs.

Youth and Impending Military Service

Up to this point we have been considering primarily the problems that youth face in normal times. It should be remembered that these problems are accentuated as youth face impending military service and that now as never before do our boys need our understanding and counsel. To be sure, many young men seem to take the prospect of such service in their stride and even to get a certain amount of enjoyment out of the uncertainty of the future. Granting that there are those for whom the thought of military service presents no particular problem, it also should be remembered that for many young people the uncertainty of the future creates in them heavy emotional burdens. It is well, therefore, that we as parents should have in mind some of the possible effects of impending military service upon our adolescent boys:

1. *The first and most obvious effect is the development of a general state either of restlessness or of lassitude.* On the one hand there is the boy who feels thwarted and confused because he cannot plan with any certainty for the future. He finds it difficult to concentrate on his studies, to get interested in his present job, or to stick long to any one task. The uncertainty of the days ahead may prove to be so emotionally upsetting that he prefers to join the service immediately in order to get the military training out of the way as soon as possible. This desire is likely to be enhanced if some of his friends are enlisting. The parents' task is to help him weigh carefully the advantages and disadvantages of immediate enlistment, leaving the final decision, of course, up to the boy but cautioning against a hasty decision.

On the other hand there is the boy who may have no particular desire to enlist now, but who nevertheless feels little incentive to effort other than that which is absolutely necessary to remain in school or to hold his present position. Such a boy may spend an inordinate amount of time in loafing and sleeping. Exasperating as such behavior will be to parents, they should recognize the reasons for it and curb their impulse to scold or deride their son for his laziness or for his inability to stick to one task.

2. *The adolescent may be plagued by certain fears which he hesitates to confess to anyone lest he be considered to be a coward.* Sometimes boys attempt to cover up their fears by extra-boisterous behavior or by a rather forced air of bravado. Remarks are likely to slip out from time to time, however, that suggest that they are more concerned than they like to admit, such remarks as, "Well, I'll probably be

six feet under the ground a year from now," or "I'll be in a foxhole within a few months." Parents certainly should not try to pry into the feelings of their boys, and many casual remarks will call for no more than a casual response on the parents' part. However, there may be occasions when we can detect that they want to talk about the future. Let us encourage them to express their misgivings; and when they do, let us not respond to their fears with a pollyanna sort of optimism or a bursting into tears. Let us face frankly with them the fact that there are dangers ahead but that the chances of survival are greater than the chances of disaster. Our own calmness and assurance will prove to be a steadying influence to them and will help to give them the assurance they need.

3. *The boy who has a physical disability that will keep him from military service is likely to experience conflicting emotions.* On the one hand there is a sense of relief that he will not need to go to war. On the other there is the despair and anguish that come from feeling that one is different from his fellows, not quite as good as they are, perhaps. For most young men it is far easier to go into military service than to be classified as a 4-F. Our task, therefore, will be to help our sons who belong in this category to realize that we understand something of the turmoil and difficulty they have in adjusting to this situation. We can encourage them to prepare well for the future and to realize that they, too, have a real contribution to make to their country, even though it may not be by means of military service.

4. *It is during adolescence that young people are striving to develop for themselves a consistent philosophy of life.* They are trying to decide what they consider to be the more significant goals and purposes of life, to determine causes to which they can give themselves unreservedly, and to make up their minds as to what ethical standards are im-

portant for persons and groups. They have been taught in the home, school, and church that the welfare of mankind depends upon the universal achievement of such virtues as honesty, justice, compassion, unselfishness, purity, and love. The prospect of military service and war, therefore, enterprises in which these virtues are likely to be discounted, makes more difficult the achievement of a consistent philosophy of life. Some respond to these conflicting viewpoints by becoming cynical and hard; others by a more or less rebellious spirit against all authority, including that of parents; and others by a new thoughtfulness that manifests itself in more mature thinking and behavior. Without preaching or trying to force their opinions upon their sons, thus disturbed, parents may profitably share with them, nevertheless, the reasons for their own philosophy of life and religious convictions.

5. *There will be unusually sensitive young men who decide that under no circumstances can they in any way support preparations for war, and therefore wish to register as conscientious objectors.* We may or may not agree with such a decision. That is not the point. What is important is that we should give our own son, if he belongs to this category, our moral and—if necessary—legal support during the trying days that are sure to follow. As has been suggested so frequently in these pages, we must encourage our boys and girls to think for themselves and to rejoice in every evidence of their growing independence of thought, even though we may not always agree with them. And let us not forget that it takes courage to be a conscientious objector.

6. *Let us not forget that girls, too, are influenced by the departure of their boy friends for military service.* They, too, become restless. They want to find a place where they can serve their country. Some may feel drawn, therefore,

to nurses' training or to service in the women's corps in one of the branches of the armed forces. The fact that many boys are in the service may somewhat curtail their social life. They will not have as many dates as they would like. There will be a tendency for bitter rivalry to develop for the attention of the boys that are left. On the other hand, should her boy friend be in the service, a girl may react by refusing to participate in social affairs. Again, let parents be sympathetic and understanding; let them provide for their daughters opportunities for wholesome social contacts and interesting creative activities. Encourage them to live as normal a life as possible and to continue to prepare themselves for future usefulness.

And now we send our boys and girls out into the world, into their own homes, into their own vocations, or perhaps into the military service of their country, to live their lives in their own way. We do so without any hesitation, as we are confident that the Christian character that they have developed during the years they have been with us will lead them to face every situation with the spirit of our Master. We know that life will be rich and full for them.

CHAPTER **12**

Becoming Successful Parents

$\mathcal{P}$ERHAPS YOU REMEMBER THE "GOOD OLD DAYS" when if a child misbehaved or developed undesirable personal characteristics people would remark, "What a disagreeable child. I feel so sorry for his parents!"

Today in a similar situation little sympathy is wasted upon the parents. Rather smugly do their fellows remark, "What a failure those parents have been. I feel sorry for the poor child. He never had a chance to develop a wholesome personality because of his parents' lack of judgment and insight into child behavior."

A Word of Comfort

It is because there is so much of truth in this latter statement that it hurts. There is no question, as has been indicated time and time again in these chapters, but that the influence of parents upon children is far greater than any other influence. In our eagerness to emphasize their influence, however, we are likely to give the impression that children are like "putty" that can be molded as parents will. Nothing could be further from the truth. Children are growing individuals with minds and wills of their own. To be sure, parents determine to a large extent the nature and direction of their growth, but this does not mean that they should consider themselves specifically responsible for everything a child does. Children themselves have something to say about how they behave. Furthermore, they are influenced by their associates, by the school, the church, and the community as well as by their parents.

There would seem to be at least a ray of comfort in all this for overconscientious parents. *Sometimes* the behavior of boys and girls is in spite of, rather than because of, our guidance of them. Sometimes we may be right and they wrong.

Parents Are Important

Throughout this book emphasis has been placed upon the influence of parents upon growing boys and girls, and suggestions have been given as to how they may best guide them. A few of these suggestions may be listed under "do" and "don't" columns. Wise parents, for example:

DO	DON'T
See to it that children have nourishing food and sufficient rest.	Nag children about eating and sleeping.
Protect children from fear-producing situatons such as exciting television and radio programs, movies and stories that are too vivid.	Pass on to children their own fears.
Guide children into successful experiences.	Expect more of children than they have a right to expect.
Give merited approval generously.	Constantly criticize children for failures or lack of popularity.
Provide playmates for children.	Give too much protection.
Respect individual differences in children.	Compare children with each other.
Help children develop socially desirable skills and graces.	Push children too rapidly into social situations.

DO	DON'T
Use their authority sparingly.	Use their authority to bolster their own egos.
Try to understand reasons for behavior before trying to deal with it.	Deal with behavior on the impulse of the moment.
Give children honest answers to their questions about sex.	Expect others to teach their children about sex.
Help children learn how to use money wisely.	Keep from their children their financial condition.
Share with children their own religious insights.	Expect the church to take over the religious guidance of their children.

Wholesome Parents

As we come to the close of this book, let us remember that:

1. *Wholesome parents tend to have wholesome children.* Wholesome parents, first of all, are those who are well adjusted in their relationship to each other. That is the reason the second chapter was devoted to this matter of parental adjustment. If affection has grown dim, if their interests separate rather than unify, and if there is jealousy and lack of understanding, the atmosphere in the home will be tense and conducive to unnecessary bickering by all the members of the family. Furthermore, husband and wife are likely to lavish on children the affection they should give to each other. The father may favor one child, the mother another. The children soon learn to play the father against the mother in order to get their wishes granted, and unwholesome personality habits are developed. The overprotective mother frequently is one who is starving for affection. The doting father may be compensating for marital unhappiness.

Wholesome parents, furthermore, are emotionally mature. They scarcely can expect their children to face reality courageously if they themselves constantly avoid it. The parent who loses his self-control, who has temper tantrums and engages in pouting, is a teacher—a bad one—of his children. Parents who face the obstacles, failures, and sorrows of life with poise, without recourse to whining, rationalizing, or despair, leave their children a heritage of inestimable value.

Wholesome parents have many interests. To be sure, they do not have so many that they neglect the home for them. Some of the most pathetic children in our communities are the "orphans" of prominent mothers and fathers whose public-spirited activities leave them little time to spend with their children. On the other hand, the mother whose only interest is in the home, or the father who is completely immersed in his business or profession, becomes intellectually stale and emotionally warped and thus is a poor companion and guide for growing boys and girls.

2. *The responsibilities of parenthood should be welcomed rather than grudgingly accepted.* Let us not assume that the parent is abnormal who occasionally is somewhat irked by the responsibilities and anxieties that accompany parenthood. The parent, however, who finds little joy in his children, who begrudges the limitation to his freedom they bring, and who impresses upon them the sacrifices he is making for them is not giving them a fair chance to develop wholesome personalities. Some of these children will develop a sense of guilt and feel insecure; others will rebel and become overly aggressive.

3. *Fathers, too, are parents!* It is increasingly realized that this task of guiding boys and girls so that they may enter adulthood with poise, confidence, self-reliance, and a vital Christian faith is too big for one parent. Furthermore,

the contribution of each parent to the life of the child is unique; neither parent can take the place of the other.

Perhaps the most glaring fault of fathers is that they get so busy they have little time to give to their children. Altogether too many children who have physical fathers are nevertheless spiritually fatherless. Sometimes fathers falsely assume they can neglect their children when they are small and yet have a fine, close relationship with them when they reach adolescence. It is exceedingly important that fathers should have a genuine interest in their children and in all that they do, that they make every effort to understand them, and that they take time to play and work with them. It is more desirable to spend a little time each day with a child than it is to give an entire day to him every week or so.

It is unfortunate that so many fathers feel ill at ease in any group studying child or adolescent development. They need to know, for example, how to use authority wisely, to build in children feelings of self-confidence, to provide wholesome sex education, to help boys and girls select their vocations, and to make religion meaningful to them.

4. *Perfectionism either for oneself or for one's children is undesirable.* All the joy is taken out of parenthood if one is a perfectionist and cannot take with at least a fair degree of equanimity the inevitable mistakes that parents are sure to make. Of course we'll make mistakes, but so what? If we really love our youngsters and are trying to do what is right, the chances are that they will survive in spite of our mistakes. If we feel we must be perfect and are in constant fear of doing something wrong, we will be in a perpetual state of tension that is not conducive to the relaxing, wholesome atmosphere to be expected in a Christian home. Furthermore, we will magnify the mistakes we do make out of all proportion to their seriousness and will

worry unduly about them. Let us not try too hard, therefore, at being a good parent. Let's get all the information and help we can, do our best, and then expect both success and failure in our relationships with our children. After all, they'd rather have us human than perfect!

5. *An intelligent, understanding love is the secret of successful parenthood.* In a Christian home we may expect that atmosphere of genuine affection, respect for personality, and sympathetic understanding that contributes to the development of wholesome personality. In a home pervaded by such an atmosphere parental mistakes, and there are certain to be some as we have just noted, do not have a devastating effect upon children. The harmful results of unwise disciplinary measures are largely nullified if the child feels secure in his parents' affections. Without this sense of security a child becomes maladjusted regardless of the technical correctness of the parents' behavior.

Intelligent love does not spoil children. It helps them develop inner disciplines and self-control. It encourages the growth of independence. It rejoices when apron strings are broken. Understanding love does not embarrass boys and girls. It helps parents to know how they think and feel. It leads to that fine spirit of comradeship that sustains and encourages them in their struggle toward adulthood. It makes a Christian home possible.

And now, may our prayer be that we may so guide our boys and girls that they will indeed grow "in wisdom and stature, and in favour with God and man." To this end may our homes be truly Christian.

Suggestions for Further Reading

IN ADDITION TO THE READINGS SUGGESTED BELOW PARENTS should consult their denominational publishing houses for lists of books and pamphlets for parents. They will also find exceedingly helpful a selected book list on family life compiled by Leland Foster Wood for the National Council of the Churches of Christ in the United States of America, 79 E. Adams, Chicago 3, Ill.

Family Life

Benedict, Agnes E., and Franklin, Adele. *The Happy Home*. New York: Appleton-Century-Crofts, Inc., 1948. Considers ways of creating a happy home with special emphasis upon parent-child relationships.

Eisenberg, Helen and Larry. *The Family Pleasure Chest*. Nashville: The Parthenon Press, 1951.

Ellenwood, James L. *There's No Place Like Home*. New York: Charles Scribner's Sons, 1938.

————. *It Runs in the Family*. New York: Charles Scribner's Sons, 1942. Practical suggestions for family life written in a popular, amusing, and thought-provoking style.

Hamilton, Mrs. Clarence H. *Doorway to a Happy Home*. Indianapolis: The Bobbs-Merrill Co., Inc., 1950. A very helpful book on family relationships.

Levy, John, and Munroe, Ruth. *The Happy Family*. New York: Alfred A. Knopf, Inc., 1938. For those who wish to probe deeper into the problems of marital adjustment and family living.

Husband-Wife Relationships

Butterfield, Oliver M. *Sex Life in Marriage*. New York: Emerson Books, Inc., 1937. One of the best books dealing with sex in marriage.

————. *Marriage and Sexual Harmony*. New York: Emerson Books, Inc., 1938. This pamphlet can also be highly recommended.

Duvall, Evelyn. *Building Your Marriage*. New York: Public Affairs Pamphlet, 1946.

Duvall, Evelyn, and Hill, Reuben. *When You Marry*. New York: Association Press, 1945.

Landis, Judson T. and Mary G. *The Marriage Handbook*. New York: Prentice-Hall, Inc., 1948. An edition for laymen of a very helpful college textbook on courtship and marriage.

Wood, Leland F. *How Love Grows in Marriage*. New York: The Macmillan Co., 1950. Illustrations of married couples who face problems constructively.

SUGGESTIONS FOR FURTHER READING

Children in the Home

Bacmeister, Rhoda W. *Growing Together.* New York: Appleton-Century-Crofts, Inc., 1947. Gives wise guidance to parents of growing children, dealing with some of the common mistakes parents make.

Baruch, Dorothy W. *New Ways in Discipline.* New York: McGraw-Hill Book Co., 1949.

Burgess, Helen S. *Discipline: What Is It?* New York: Child Study Association of America, Inc., 1948. An excellent discussion of discipline.

Dunbar, Flanders. *Your Child's Mind and Body.* New York: Random House, 1949. Deals with practical problems parents face such as children's fears, health, and their attitudes toward sex.

Gesell, Arnold. *The Child from Five to Ten.* New York: Harper & Brothers, 1946. Considers the behavior of preschool and school children as they develop year by year. Helpful if parents realize that individual differences in maturing may cause some children to deviate from exact pattern of growth described.

Gesell, Arnold, et al. *Infant and Child in the Culture of Today.* New York: Harper & Brothers, 1943.

Gruenberg, Sidonie. *We, the Parents.* New York: Harper & Brothers, 1939. Excellent consideration of such problems as discipline, the use of money, explaining the facts of birth and death.

Gruenberg, Sidonie, et al. *Parents' Questions.* New York: Harper & Brothers, 1947. Deals in a helpful way with questions parents have asked including those about discipline and authority, emotional development, sex education, and character and spiritual growth.

Hymes, James L. *Enjoy Your Child—Ages 1, 2, and 3.* New York: Public Affairs Pamphlet, 1948.

Keliher, Alice. *Life and Growth.* New York: Appleton-Century-Crofts, Inc., 1938.

Lambert, Clara. *Understand Your Child—From 6 to 12.* New York: Public Affairs Pamphlet, 1948.

Powdermaker, Florence, and Grimes, Louise. *Children in the Family.* New York: Farrar & Rhinehart, Inc., 1940. Helpful suggestions for dealing with the everyday problems in the home.

Ridenour, Nina. *Some Special Problems of Children.* New York: National Mental Health Foundation, 1949. Excellent consideration of such problems as fears, aggressions, destructiveness, and masturbation.

Spock, Benjamin. *The Pocket Book of Baby and Child Care.* New York: Pocket Books, Inc., 1946. A popular and reliable guide.

Strang, Ruth. *A Study of Young Children.* New York and Nashville: Abingdon Press, 1944.

Teagarden, Florence. *Child Psychology for Professional Workers.* New York: Prentice-Hall, Inc., 1940.

Wieman, Regina. *Does Your Child Obey?* New York: Harper & Brothers,

1943. Makes a distinction between constructive and destructive obedience.

Your Child from One to Six. Washington, D.C.: Children's Bureau, Social Security Administration. Inexpensive and exceedingly helpful.

Your Child from Six to Twelve. Washington, D.C.: Children's Bureau, Social Security Administration. Very helpful.

Concerning Adolescents

Duvall, Evelyn. *Keeping Up with Teen-Agers.* New York: Public Affairs Pamphlet, 1947.

Elliott, Grace. *Understanding the Adolescent Girl.* New York: Woman's Press, 1949.

Strain, Frances Bruce. *But You Don't Understand.* New York: Appleton-Century-Crofts, Inc., 1950. Helps parents understand the problems teen-agers face.

Taylor, Katharine W. *Understanding and Guiding the Adolescent Child.* New York: Grosset & Dunlap, 1948. Reprint of the book, *Do Adolescents Need Parents?* Very valuable.

Thom, Douglas. *Guiding the Adolescent.* Washington, D. C.: Children's Bureau, Social Security Administration. A pamphlet all parents of adolescents should secure.

Sex Education

Burkhart, Roy. *From Friendship to Marriage.* New York: Harper & Brothers, 1937.

Clapp, Emily V. *Growing Up in the World Today.* The Massachusetts Society for Social Hygiene, 1946. One of the best pamphlets in the field for boys and girls in their teens.

Dahlberg, Edwin. *Youth and the Homes of Tomorrow.* Philadelphia: Judson Press, 1934.

De Schweinitz, Karl. *Growing Up.* New York: The Macmillan Co., 1928. Continues to be one of the most helpful books for parents of children six to ten years of age.

Dickerson, Roy E. *So Youth May Know.* New York: Association Press, rev. 1948.

Duvall, Evelyn. *Facts of Life and Love for Teenagers.* New York: Association Press, 1950. Especially helpful for teen-agers.

Eddy, George. *Sex and Youth.* London: Student Christian Movement Press, Ltd., 1937.

Edson, Newell W. *From Boy to Man.* New York: American Social Hygiene Association. A helpful pamphlet for boys of 11 or older.

Elliott, Grace, and Bone, Harry. *The Sex Life of Youth.* New York: Association Press, 1929.

Health for Girls. New York: American Social Hygiene Association. Especially helpful for teen-age girls.

Hymes, James L. *How to Tell Your Child About Sex*. New York: Public Affairs Pamphlet, 1949.

Strain, Frances Bruce. *Being Born*. New York: D. Appleton-Century Co., Inc., 1936. Deals wholesomely with the facts of human reproduction for boys and girls of junior high school age.

———. *Love at the Threshold*. New York: Appleton-Century-Crofts, Inc., 1942.

———. *New Patterns in Sex Teaching*. New York: D. Appleton-Century Co., Inc., 1934. Although one of the older books in this field, it is one of the most helpful in suggesting answers to children's questions about sex.

When Children Ask About Sex. New York: Child Study Association of America, Inc., 1943.

The Family and Religion

Bailey, Albert. *The Gospel in Art*. Boston: Pilgrim Press, 1931.

Baxter, Edna M. *Children and the Changing World*. New York and Nashville: Abingdon Press, 1942. Considers ways by which children may be helped to become sensitive to the Christian demands in the fields of brotherhood, temperance, and labor and management.

Bowie, Walter Russell. *The Bible Story for Boys and Girls* (Old Testament). New York and Nashville: Abingdon Press, 1952. Should be in the library of every home where there are children.

———. *The Bible Story for Boys and Girls* (New Testament). New York and Nashville: Abingdon Press, 1951.

———. *The Story of the Bible*. New York and Nashville: Abingdon Press, 1934. For children aged 9 to 11. Older children probably will find it interesting also.

Bro, Margueritte Harmon. *When Children Ask*. Chicago: Willett, Clark & Co., 1940. Deals in a fascinating way with questions concerning God, prayer, death, babies, and the inequalities in society.

Chaplin, Dora P. *Children and Religion*. New York: Charles Scribner's Sons, 1948. Helpful advice concerning religious instruction of children.

Curtis, Muriel S. *Christianity Begins at Home*. New York: The National Council of Churches of Christ in the United States of America, 1949. Specific suggestions for family activities.

Gebhard, Anna L. *Enjoying the Bible at Home*. St. Louis: Bethany Press, 1951. Gives specific suggestions as to how the Bible may be used in the home.

Jones, Mary Alice. *Guiding Children in Christian Growth*. New York and Nashville: Abingdon Press, 1949. Considers how religious growth may be guided in the home and in the church.

McGavran, Grace W. *And When You Pray*. Boston: Pilgrim Press, 1941.

Milton, Jennie Lou. *Teaching a Little Child to Pray*. Nashville: Board of Education of The Methodist Church, 1943. This pamphlet should be in the hands of all parents of small children.

Moody, Mildred, and Eakin, Frank. *Your Child's Religion.* New York: The Macmillan Co., 1942. Suggests ways of helping children develop religious concepts.

Roorbach, Rosemary. *What Bible Story Books Should Children Have?* Chicago: International Council of Religious Education, 1949.

Rosser, Pearl R. *Your Child Grows Toward God.* Philadelphia: Judson Press, 1944. Helps parents understand ideas of God children may comprehend at different ages.

Smither, Ethel. *The Use of the Bible with Children.* New York and Nashville: Abingdon Press, 1937.

Staples, Ethlyne and Edward. *Children in a Christian Home.* New York and Nashville: Abingdon Press, 1948. Excellent suggestions for guiding the religious growth of children.

Sweet, Herman J. *Opening the Door for God.* Philadelphia: Westminster Press, 1944. Suggestions for use of the Bible and worship in the home.

Thomas, Mazelle W. *The Family Worships Together.* Boston: Pilgrim Press, 1949. Unusually helpful suggestions for family worship.

Welker, Edith F., and Barber, Aimée A. *Thoughts of God for Boys and Girls.* Hartford: Connecticut Council of Churches and Religious Education.

Wieman, Regina. *The Family Lives Its Religion.* New York: Harper & Brothers, 1941.